MW00640316

PRAISE FOR *THINK LIKE JESUS*

Dave and Ashley carry a breadth of wisdom that is deeply life-giving. Their love for the Scriptures and for people blend powerfully to result in teaching that both lifts eyes to possibility and at the same time practically gives feet their next steps. I am grateful that this book will be a resource to my teenagers, and I look forward to borrowing it after they've finished reading it.

DAN LIAN

Associate Pastor of NewSpring Church (Anderson, SC)

Dave has written a book that shares the wisdom he has modeled as long as I've known him. This book will help you trust God and live out your faith in matters that all of us wrestle with like "What is God's will for my life," "How can be happier," "What choice should I make," and countless others. I can't think of anyone better to help the teens and young adults in my life."

JASON ISAACS

Pastor of Hope City Church, Author of *I Want What God Wants*.

The challenges that young people face are vast. Our thoughts are tremendous forces. Now more than ever, we need resources that can teach teenagers and young adults how to think critically and creatively—like Jesus!

JOSIAH KENNEALY

Pastor, Author, and Host of the *Young Adults Today Podcast*

In my teens, my dad had our family read the chapter of Proverbs that matched up with the date. We did this for years. I can't even begin to explain how much unnecessary suffering those Proverbs have saved me from in my life. The wisdom of King Solomon is a key to a lifetime of success. That's why I love the practical and immediately applicable insight my friend Dave has written in this book. Read it now and reap the benefits of Proverbs for a lifetime.

JOËL MALM

Founder of Summit Leaders, Author of *Love Slows Down*

One thing is for certain, you will never regret investing in yourself now for the sake of a better future you. I certainly wish I had done more of that as a young adult. Dave Willis phenomenally and practically guides you through the Proverbs as he breaks them down in palatable, impactful ways. This devotional will be life-changing for your walk with God and ability to love the season you are in!

KAIT WARMAN

National Best-Selling Author, Dating Coach, Founder of Heart of Dating

This book will help strengthen and challenge your walk with Jesus. You will love this devotional!

RAY GREEN

Lead Pastor of Immanuel Baptist Church (Lexington, KY)

You can't force teens or young adults to love God's Word, but Dave Willis' devotional will help them—through insight, humor, and readability—to appreciate its wisdom and beauty.

MICHAEL ROWNTREE

Lead Pastor of Wellspring Church, Co-Host of The Remnant Radio

The devotional is incredible! We LOVE it! We will be ordering dozens and passing them out to all the young adults we know!

DON AND SUZANNE MANNING

Hosts of the *Crazy Cool Family Podcast*

THINK
LIKE
JESUS

FOR YOUNG ADULTS

LIFE LESSONS FROM PROVERBS

BESTSELLING AUTHOR
DAVE WILLIS

CONTENTS

DEDICATION

This book is dedicated to my wonderful sons: Cooper, Connor, Chandler, and Chatham. Your mom and I love you very much, and we are honored to be your parents. As you grow, we pray you always follow Jesus and walk in the path of wisdom. The Lord has wonderful plans for you.

My sons, do not forget this teaching and keep these commands in your hearts. They will add many years of peace and prosperity to your lives. Always pursue love and faithfulness. Keep them in your heart, and you will earn favor and a good name in the sight of God and people.

Proverbs 3:1–4

INTRODUCTION

Honestly, it doesn't seem like that was very long ago that I was a young adult. In many ways, it seems like just yesterday. I know, I know, that sounds like such an "old guy" thing to say, but I can't help it.

Right now, I'm a dad of four sons. Two of them are already teenagers, and two are in elementary school. Our youngest son just turned six-years-old, and last week he almost burned our house down. Seriously.

We had some friends over for dinner, and my wife, Ashley, had the entire house looking amazing. She had a scented candle burning in our bathroom inside a decorative metal cylinder to give the room a little atmosphere. The candle also helped disguise some of the nasty smells that can fill our bathroom. One of our guests walked into the bathroom and shouted out, "Wow! There's a huge fire in here!"

We rushed into the bathroom, and the metal cylinder with the scented candle inside had flames shooting out of it like a blow torch! We quickly carried the flaming cylinder outside and threw water on it until it stopped. Our neighbors probably thought we were crazy and having a bonfire in our front yard in the middle of winter.

We came back into the house and started trying to figure out what had caused the fire. We asked the kids if anyone had done anything to the candle and our five-year-old slowly raised his hand with a look of shame and embarrassment on his face. We asked him what happened, and he said he threw toilet paper into the metal cylinder to watch the fire burn brighter.

With some firmness and frustration in my voice, I said, "Buddy, that wasn't a good choice. When we're outside together at the fire pit, you can put wood and sticks in the fire as long as I'm there with you, but we never ever put something on a candle inside a house because it could burn the house down."

He looked at me with a quivering lip and innocence in his voice and said, "But daddy, you never teached me that before."

He was right (even though grammatically speaking, "teached" isn't a real word). I had never taught him this lesson, so he tried to figure out the rules about fire on his own. Thankfully, no serious damage happened, and he'll remember the lesson the next time he wants to throw toilet paper on an open flame.

As a young adult, you face daily choices and temptations that have the potential to burn you. You've probably already seen friends who have made unwise decisions that have had serious consequences. Maybe you've made some of those decisions in your own life too.

Those decisions—and life in general—can feel complicated, but I've got some really good news for you. You have a loving Father in Heaven who wants to make sure you learn all the right lessons to help you live the best life possible. He wants to prevent you from having to make mistakes that will cause you harm or wreck your future. Even when you do make mistakes, He wants you to know you have a path to forgiveness and healing.

These life lessons are outlined in a book of the Bible called Proverbs. I started reading Proverbs as a teenager, and it totally transformed the way I saw God, the way I saw myself, and the way I approached life's biggest choices. Learning these lessons at that age has proved to be one of God's most important gifts in my life, so I wanted to create this resource specifically for you, so you could experience the same life-changing gift of His wisdom.

Every verse of Proverbs, the Bible's most condensed collection of practical life tools, holds the power to infuse your life with more wisdom. Since the reign of King Solomon, for the past 3,000 years, these words have guided people on the path of wisdom. Proverbs holds a treasure trove of divine insights that can deeply enrich every aspect of your life, your faith, your finances, your relationships, and your future.

Here's the best part... King Solomon wrote Proverbs primarily for young adults! That's right, teens and young adults were King Solomon's primary audience. God wanted to make sure you had a customized instruction manual for life included in the Bible, and if you'll apply it in adolescence and early adulthood, it will keep you on the right track all your life.

I called this book *Think Like Jesus* because the Proverbs would have clearly been a vital part of Jesus' upbringing as a first-century Jewish boy. As a teenager, Jesus would have studied the Proverbs along with other parts of Scripture. Jesus' life, ministry, and teachings have deep roots in the timeless wisdom of the Old Testament Scriptures, and you can see many references to the Proverbs throughout all four Gospels. Faced with tough decisions, Jesus always made the right choice. He wants you to have the tools to make the right choices too.

As you go through the thirty-one daily devotions in this book, I encourage you to think about the daily Scripture, reflect on the thoughts I've included, and then take time to pray. As you go through these devotions, ask yourself, "What should I *do* in my life as a response to this Scripture? What decisions should I be making in school, in my hobbies, in my relationships, and in every part of my life based on what God is teaching me?"

I pray this devotional brings you into a stronger relationship with your family and friends and into a more intimate relationship with Jesus. I also pray that this devotional will launch a lifelong love for God's Word, which will continue to shape your faith and your life after you've finished this devotional. God has good things in store for you! His plans for your life are bigger and better than anything you can imagine.

I'm so excited for you to start this journey because I know first-hand what a life-changing impact it can have to learn these principles as a young adult. You're already showing wisdom beyond your years, just taking the time to invest in yourself by reading this book. I believe that God is going to do something very special in your life and your faith over the next thirty-one days. Let's get started!

DAY 1 March 25, 2023

Wisdom vs. Foolishness

"Obedience to God is the foundation of true wisdom, but foolish people hate God's timeless truths."

Proverbs 1:7

One of the main themes in the Book of Proverbs is the difference between a wise person and a fool. It might sound harsh to call anyone a "fool," and if you went around your school calling people a fool or calling your siblings fools, you'd probably get in trouble fast. However, the Bible wants to make sure we can recognize foolish behavior when we see it (especially when we see it in ourselves).

God wants us to know that we have a choice before us daily. We can choose one of two paths: a narrow road that follows God's wisdom or a broad road of destructive foolishness full of every counterfeit option the world can provide. Every day, you will face temptations to choose a foolish, dead-end road or to choose a path that leads to wisdom, honor, and health. Even the choices that seem small, like what kind of music to listen to, what to post on your social media, and where to hang out with your friends, can have a big impact on pushing you toward more wisdom or more foolishness.

We all have the opportunity to be a fool in one or more parts of our life. Foolishness and wisdom have nothing to do with educational level, social status, or age. Fools can be young or old, male or female, educated or uneducated, rich or poor. You can't tell a fool from the outward appearance, but a fool will always reveal his or her foolishness through their words and actions.

A fool lives as though he or she answers to nobody. A wise person knows we always answer to God and to the human authorities God has placed in our lives. A fool rolls their eyes at discipline and treats all forms of discipline as a prison. A wise person welcomes discipline and knows it brings greater freedom and influence. A fool can't be taught anything because he thinks he's already smarter than everybody. A wise person humbly knows that he always has more to learn, and every person, every situation, and even every mistake can be a good teacher.

As we begin this journey through the timeless wisdom in the book of Proverbs, make a commitment to yourself and to God to have a humble and teachable spirit. A humble heart and a teachable attitude will give you a huge head start toward wisdom. Foolishness is the lie that tells you you already know everything. Learning doesn't stop at graduation. Even after you finish school, God wants you to keep learning from Him all your life. Wisdom and learning are lifelong pursuits.

The path to lifelong wisdom begins with trusting God and following His plan. Some translations use the phrase, "The fear of the Lord is the beginning of wisdom," which sounds confusing because the word "fear" might make you think you should just be afraid of God all the time. But, to "fear the Lord" just means to show respect to God for His awesome power and love and to show obedience to God's plans for you. It basically means we need to respect God and His Word and trust His Word even more than we trust our own feelings.

While we should have this kind of respect for the Lord, we should also remember that because of what Jesus has done for us, we can also approach God as a friend. Once you put your faith in Jesus, God adopts you into His family as a son or a daughter. God claims you as one of His kids, and He loves you more than you can imagine. When you have the right kind of fear of the Lord, God gives you the strength and courage to not have fear about the future or anything else.

Remember that God's love motivates everything God ever tells you to do because He wants you to live a great life. He wants to guide you through your life as your best friend and someone you can always count on. He has such great plans for you! Those plans include walking in His wisdom every day.

PRAYER FOR TODAY

———

Father, thank You for showing us the path to wisdom. There's a lot in my life and my world that I don't completely understand right now, so I know I need Your wisdom. I know that the decisions I make right now will shape my future, so help me choose wisely. Please give me the strength to overcome temptation and surround me with friends who will be a positive influence. Help me have the wisdom to be a positive influence on others as well. Give me the wisdom to be a blessing to my family, my school, my friends, and everyone in my life. Help me make decisions today that my future self will celebrate. Today, I'm choosing to walk on the path of wisdom instead of the path of foolishness. Help me stay on the right path every day.

In Jesus's name, amen.

A humble heart and a teachable attitude will give you a huge head start toward wisdom.

DAY 2 April 1, 2023

God's Will for Your Life

"Trust God with all your heart. Trust Him more than you trust in yourself. If you'll seek His will in all you do, He will show you which paths to take."

Proverbs 3:5-6

You've reached a time of life where there are BIG decisions in your near future. Where should I go to college? What do I want to do with my life? Should I date that person or not? When should I get married?

So many young people (and old people too) live paralyzed by the fear of making wrong decisions and somehow wrecking their lives. I have very good news for you: God doesn't want you living worried about the future. He cares more about your life than you do, and He won't lead you down the wrong roads when you do your best to follow Him with a sincere heart.

Still, it's important to approach life's big decisions with wisdom. Seeking *God's will* for our lives is about so much than trying to discern whether God wants us to choose Option A or Option B. We must remember that God primarily wants us to develop our character to become more like Christ as we live in a healthy relationship with Him and with people. When a Pharisee asked Jesus which commandment was the most important (he thought he was sneaky), Jesus essentially said, "Love God with all your heart and love people" (Matthew 22:37–40, Mark 12:29–31).

Some people spend their whole life trying to figure out God's will, but that's not the best approach. The Bible never once tells us to "figure it out," but over and over it tells us to trust God—He's already got it all figured out.

God's will for your life is for you to be committed to following His word, love Him, love other people, and become more like Jesus every day. When I say love, by the way, I don't mean the romantic term. Love means being willing to serve people and recognizing the sacred, God-given value in all people—including yourself.

If you'll make love your primary mission, then you'll already be living God's will. We don't approach God only when we come to a crossroads where we don't know whether to turn right or left. We walk every step with Jesus, so when we do come to a crossroads, He gently guides us toward the right path.

Even when you miss a step, He works all things together for your good. If your heart's desire is to know Him and grow closer to Him, then He'll work His will in you and through you in every season of your life. When we rebel and defiantly choose the wrong path, once we turn back to Him, He is right there to help us start where we are and get to where we need to be.

God still cares about the decisions of your life. You should still pray and ask: Which job should I take? Whom should I date? What should I study in school? Which activities are the best fit for my time and talents?

God cares even more than you do about the details of your life, but He also cares about YOU. He doesn't want you living with anxiety, agonizing over every decision as if you're one missed opportunity away from ruining His plans for you. Remember, God only wants you to know Him and love Him, and that can happen from anywhere.

Start right where you are. Commit your current situation to Him. Promise to prioritize your relationship with Him and keep learning from Him through His word and prayer. Choose gratitude for your current situation, knowing God will bring good things out of it (even the hard parts). If you'll do these things, you can stand right in the middle of God's presence and His will for your life. If He needs to move you somewhere, He will let you know when and where in His perfect timing.

PRAYER FOR TODAY

———

Lord, help me to put You first. I know that's Your will for my life. Help me trust You with every decision. Guide me where You want and help me choose contentment if Your current plan is for me to stay right where I am. Use me here. I know my life is never on hold, even if it feels like I'm in a waiting season. You're always moving. You're always working things together for our good. Thank You for loving me. I commit to trusting You with every part of my life and every decision. I know You're in control, that You have incredible plans for my life, and that You'll guide me where I need to go. Thank You for all You're doing, and for all You're going to do. Please give me the patience to trust in Your plan and in Your timing.

In Jesus's name, amen.

The Bible never once tells us to "figure it out," but over and over it tells us to trust God—He's already got it all figured out.

DAY 3 April 8, 2023

Keep Moving Forward

———

"Stay focused. Keep your eye on the prize. Keep moving forward. Make sure you keep heading in the right direction and don't get sidetracked by sin or distracted by frivolous detours."

Proverbs 4:25–27

I grew up in Kentucky, surrounded by horse farms. My family never owned any horses, but I always had a fascination for these powerful and majestic animals. Watching a racehorse run is watching one of God's masterpieces in motion.

A Thoroughbred racehorse is one of the most powerful and magnificent creatures on the earth, but it has a significant weak spot. With their eyes on the sides of their heads, Thoroughbreds have a broad field of peripheral vision. That field of vision in itself seems like a good defense mechanism, but it also provides all kinds of distractions. It makes it nearly impossible for the horse to run in a straight line or to keep his eyes focused straight ahead.

For a horse to run in a race, he must be trained. He must wear blinders which drastically limit his field of vision to force his eyes to stay focused on the path in front of him. With training and focus, he becomes capable of being one of the world's elite racers.

Humans have some similar distractions. We're also prone to let our eyes wander from the path in front of us—predisposed to getting sidetracked. We normally justify these small course detours by thinking they won't make a significant difference. When we do this, we forget that a ship whose course is off by only a few degrees on a transatlantic journey will eventually end up hundreds of miles off-course. A few degrees, over time, can mean landing in Cuba when you were aiming for Canada.

The Bible teaches us to run the race set before us, keeping our eyes on Jesus, the one who keeps us on course. When you follow Jesus, you're always headed in the right direction. If you've gotten out of step with Him, even the smallest detours can create significant problems over time.

Horses don't know when they've started walking in the wrong direction, but God has given you the mind and a soul a horse doesn't possess. If you feel off track in any part of your life right now, then it's time to make a decision to turn back to God and start heading in the right direction again.

In life, these moments of being "sidetracked" can happen through sin when we pursue toxic forces and give in to temptation. Being sidetracked can also occur through more innocent means, like when our hobbies or our smartphones start slowly taking up too much time, keeping us away from family or our studies. It can happen when we stop prioritizing a daily quiet time with the Lord. There are countless ways to get sidetracked, but God will always guide us back home.

Jesus doesn't shout at us every time we step out of line like a mean boss. He's our loving friend and Savior who gently corrects us like a good shepherd who patiently brings a lost sheep back into the safety of his care. Sometimes a sheep doesn't even know it's lost, and sometimes a person doesn't realize he or she has gotten off-course. That's why you must stay aware of your thoughts, your schedule, and your motives at all times.

Think about what's happening in your life frequently so you'll always have an awareness of any potential blind spots that might pull you off course and take your eyes off Jesus. Stay in constant communication with God. When sin or even an innocent mistake have sidetracked you, ask Jesus to guide you back to the right path. He always will.

PRAYER FOR TODAY

Jesus, please help me stay in step with You. Help me to follow You instead of going my own way and then asking You to "bless" my efforts. I know You're the leader, not me. When I'm following You, I'm always headed in the right direction. Please reveal to me the places in my life that are currently out of sync with You. Give me the wisdom and courage to surrender these areas to You and be willing to do things Your way. I know Your plans for me are perfect. Help me keep my eyes focused on You and on the path of wisdom You're teaching me. Give me the strength to walk with You one step at a time, trusting in Your leading and Your timing.

In Jesus's name, amen.

Think about what's happening in your life frequently so you'll always have an awareness of any potential blind spots that might pull you off course and take your eyes off Jesus.

DAY 4 April 15, 2023

Work Hard

———

"If you're prone to laziness, you should learn a lesson from the ants. Their work ethic can teach you some wisdom! They don't have a boss or a ruler to force them to work, but they still work hard all summer long, storing food for the winter. Some lazy people spend more time looking for naps than they spend looking for productive work. Dodging work and sleeping during work time is the foolish path to poverty. If you live a lazy life, scarcity will haunt you, and it will be your own fault."

Proverbs 6:6–11

My great-grandfather was the hardest working man I ever knew. He lost his father very young, and during his teenage years in the Great Depression, he worked to provide for himself and for his mother. He eventually married and raised eight children on a farm he ran through long hours of hard, manual labor. He once pulled his own tooth out with a rusty pair of pliers because he didn't want to miss a day of harvesting to go into town to see a dentist. A hardworking man, he left his family a legacy of faith, love, and discipline.

You've grown up in a time when technology and on-demand access to things have made life easier than it has been for many of those who came before you. All of this new technology has great benefits, but one possible side effect is that it can take away a sense of the importance of hard work. We tend to rely on computers and robots to do the work so we can relax and do what we want. Even with all the technological tools at your fingertips, life still requires a lot of hard work, and you will have to work hard to fulfill God's plans for you.

God wants us to rest when it's time to rest, but He also commands us to work when it's time to work. In Proverbs 6, God shows us that tiny little ants have a better work ethic than a lot of people. They work hard, and as a result, they have what they need. If you'll choose to work hard in your studies and in all parts of your life, that hard work will pay off in big ways.

Maybe your parents have disciplined you in the past by giving you extra work as a punishment, but hard work is not a punishment. Working hard and using our God-given gifts to be industrious can bless others and ourselves. We can use our hard work as an act of worship since the New Testament tells us to work hard at everything as if every job—including school—we complete is for God Himself and not for human bosses, teachers, or parents.

Choosing to be a hard worker is one of the most important decisions you'll ever make. Hard work gives its own reward because it provides you with the grit and resilience necessary to succeed in life. Hard work also provides a safety net and removes unnecessary financial stress. Once you start working for money, having a solid work ethic will set you apart in the workplace and paves the way for promotions and better pay. Like everything God commands you to do, having a disciplined work ethic is for your own good. It gives you freedom and security as an expression of your faith and an investment in your future.

PRAYER FOR TODAY

Father, thank You for giving me the ability to work hard in my studies and in all parts of my life. I know my willingness to work hard and do my best honors You and helps me prepare for my future. Please give me the discipline to see hard work as a privilege and not as a prison. While I know work is a good thing, Father, help me to never look for my identity in my grades or my performance. Help me find my identity in You alone and not in anything else. Guide my steps to all the work You've prepared for me to do and help me do it with joy.

In Jesus's name, amen.

Hard work gives its own reward because it provides you with the grit and resilience necessary to succeed in life.

DAY 5 April 22, 2023

What God Hates

"God hates six things and seven things he truly detests: eyes that look down on other people, a tongue that speaks lies, hands that shed innocent blood, a heart that harbors evil motives, feet that run into sin, a dishonest witness who brings false accusations, and a person who intentionally brings drama and division into a family."

Proverbs 6:16–19

I f you knew God hated something, I'll bet you'd try not to do it. Right? If you knew God hated cheating on tests, would you study harder and make sure you made your grades the honest way? If you knew God hated gossip, would you be more careful in the words you said about other people? If you knew God hated sexual immorality, would you make different choices with what you watched on TV and what images you looked at online?

God is all about love, so some people are surprised to learn in Scripture that God is capable of hate. They scratch their heads in confusion, wondering how an all-loving God could hate anything. The Bible teaches us that precisely because God so fully loves His children, He's able to so fiercely hate those things that harm his children.

In Proverbs 6, this list of some of the things God hates gives us a window into the mind and heart of our loving heavenly Father. Each item that God hates is an action that directly harms His children and attempts to sabotage God's blessings for His children. Each item on this list hurts people, and God hates things that hurt people.

God hates eyes that look down on other people because He created all people in His image with dignity and eternal significance. God hates a tongue that speaks lies because it's the truth that sets us free. God hates hands that shed innocent blood because He never wants His children to suffer needless harm. He hates a heart that harbors evil motives because such a heart makes no room for Jesus, our only Savior and Lord. He hates feet that run into sin because sin hurts everyone. He hates a dishonest witness because lies always hurt people. He hates it when someone stirs up drama and division in a family because God desires that His children live together in love and unity.

Think about it this way … there's not one person in your school, in your family, in your church, or in your community who isn't loved by

God. He created every person in His image, and each one has eternal value. Jesus loved each person enough to give His own life to save them.

Since God loves people (including you) so much, we should love people too. Since God hates things that hurt people, we should hate those things too. Hating what God hates doesn't mean we should walk around in a negative or judgmental way. It's really the opposite. When we hate injustice and our hearts break over the things that hurt people, it will motivate us to lovingly and boldly work to make this world a better place.

PRAYER FOR TODAY

———

Lord, help heal our broken world. When we look around at all the injustices in our world, it's heartbreaking. I know it breaks Your heart too. Help me, Lord, to not get caught in the kinds of activities You hate. Help me instead do what You love. Help me fight for justice. Help me serve others. Help me point people toward Your grace and Your truth. Help me be an authentic example of faith in a world that needs You more than ever. Thank You for Your amazing love and grace.

In Jesus's name, amen.

The Bible teaches us that precisely because God so fully loves His children, He's able to so fiercely hate those things that harm his children.

DAY 6 *May 13, 2023*

How to Be Happy

"Wise people are joyful people, so look for wisdom in all times and in all places. Everyone who finds wisdom finds life and receives blessings from the Lord."

Proverbs 8:34–35

One of the happiest people I knew growing up was an old man named John who attended our church. Poor, the little money he did have came from the hard work of walking around town and digging through trash to fish out aluminum cans he could sell to the recycling center for a few pennies each. He didn't have any teeth but always had a quick smile to show off his grin. He had discovered a secret in life few people ever find: True happiness isn't rooted in your circumstances; it's rooted in your faith.

God wants you to live a great life. It won't always be an easy life, but it should be full of joy even on difficult days. You'll still face disappointments, losses, and even heartbreaks, but because of Jesus, you can have peace and joy through it all. Joy is happiness in its purest form, a gift from God that guards your heart in a world of negativity. "A happy heart is good medicine—but a broken spirit dries the bones" (Proverbs 17:22).

One of the greatest lies the world has ever believed is that to follow God with all your heart, you have to stop having fun. This inaccurate stereotype of faithful Christians has been perpetuated by centuries of paintings and sculptures showing saints and Christian martyrs with stern expressions and painful grimaces on their faces. These old paintings and statues might make you think grumpy, mean-looking people fill the history of Christianity. This misconception is dangerously inaccurate.

The Christian life (and life in general) can have its fair share of trials and pain. Jesus Himself even experienced great pains on earth, but He never lost His joy, and as His followers, we shouldn't either. The Holy Spirit brings love, joy, peace, patience, kindness, goodness, faithfulness, gentleness, and self-control into the hearts and lives of all who follow Jesus. The Bible tells us the joy of the Lord is our strength, a strength that's greater than any negative circumstances this life can throw our way.

Wisdom and joy might seem like two separate roads on the Christian journey, but this Scripture reminds us they are one and the same. The path of wisdom leads to joy, and the path of joy leads to wisdom. As we seek joy, we'll also find wisdom. As we seek wisdom, we'll also find joy.

King Solomon wrote most of the Proverbs. The Bible tells us he had more wisdom than anyone on earth, but that wasn't always the case. The wisdom entrusted to Solomon was given as a gift. The Bible tells the story of young Solomon preparing to inherit the throne left by his father, King David. God told Solomon he could ask for anything, and it would be granted to him. Instead of riches or power, Solomon humbly asked for the wisdom a good and faithful leader would need.

God was so pleased with Solomon's heart for wisdom that he made Solomon the wisest ruler of all time. In addition, God granted Solomon great wealth and power. Because Solomon valued wisdom first, God granted him everything else in addition to wisdom. Solomon had joy, and Solomon had wisdom, and both his joy and his wisdom were gifts from God.

Tragically, Solomon did not always use his wisdom to make wise decisions. He was still prone to selfishness and sin and had times when he disregarded the wisdom God had given to him and made foolish decisions. He sinned sexually. He sinned with pride and greed. He sinned by allowing others to lead his heart away from God.

When he chose to sin and ignored his wisdom, he invited chaos into his life and sabotaged his joy. Solomon experienced and caused a lot of unnecessary pain by straying from the path of wisdom. When we stray from the path of wisdom, we invite the same kinds of pain into our own lives. When we forget wisdom, we will inevitably lose joy in the process.

Thankfully, God is a God of grace. Once we confess our sin and turn back to Him, He quickly forgives us, and we start on the path toward healing. The healing journey can still be painful as we deal with the natural consequences our sin may have caused, but even in this discomfort,

God mercifully leads us and carries our troubles for us.

Keep pursuing wisdom and keep embracing the joy God wants all of His children to experience. If you've blown it (like we all have) and you've walked away from the path of wisdom, you don't have to stay on that dead-end road. Choose today to recommit your life to God and His ways. Embrace the joy He wants you to experience. It only takes one moment to fall into sin, but thankfully, it only takes one moment to repent and get back on the right road.

PRAYER FOR TODAY

Father, thank You for the joy You give to Your children. Let my happiness be rooted in You and not in things like my appearance, my grades, or anything else. Thank You that You offer mercy and grace when we stray from the path of wisdom. Please help me stay on the right path. Help me live a life of joy. I know in a world with so much brokenness and superficial happiness, true joy points people to You. Help me embody that kind of contagious joy that turns the skeptical hearts of those around me toward wanting a life-giving relationship with You. Thank You for the wisdom and joy You make available to all who will follow You.

In Jesus's name, amen.

True happiness isn't rooted in your circumstances; it's rooted in your faith.

DAY 7 May 20, 2023

Pride and Humility

———

"Pride and arrogance lead to destruction, but a humble heart invites wisdom."

Proverbs 11:2

Are there any people at your school or in your life who seem to walk around like they're better than everybody else? When people create cliques based on superficial factors like physical appearance, athletic ability, wealth, or any other factor, it can create insecurity both for the people inside the clique and those outside it. When someone is cocky or prideful, they can push people away and make people uncomfortable. Pride often masks insecurity. It is the enemy of love because it sabotages relationships.

Pride is a very different thing from confidence. As Christians, we should have the most confidence on earth. We should have confidence in our calling. We should have confidence in God's promises. We should have confidence that God will never leave us or forsake us. Since our confidence is rooted in God and not in ourselves, we can (and should) be simultaneously confident and humble. Jesus can only take up residence in a humble heart. He won't compete with our sinful pride.

Pride is the arrogant voice that chases away correction, reason, wisdom, and even chases away God Himself. Pride convinces us we don't need to listen to others. Pride puffs us up with an identity built on superficial and temporary circumstances. Pride undoes relationships and wrecks lives.

Pride will ruin your life and then, ironically, make you too proud to admit you've committed any failure at all. Though pride is the cause of so much destruction, it blinds its victims to their own downfall's real cause, then manipulates that person to blame his downfall on other people and other factors. Remember, "Pride inevitably leads to your own downfall" (Proverbs 16:18).

Don't chase accolades or seek the spotlight. Allow God to put you in those places of honor in His timing. Otherwise, you'll get there with the wrong motives, and your pride will sabotage any good you could have accomplished with your influence. Don't go through life strutting around trying to convince others of your importance or making popularity your goal. Your importance isn't rooted in popularity; it's rooted in God, and He already loves you unconditionally.

When you let go of pride, you can open your hands and heart to experience the full life of wisdom God wants you to live. When you give up the need to build your own image, Christ can form you more completely into His image. When you surrender your need for control, you tap into God's power to control your circumstances for the better.

Don't ever mistake humility with weakness. Jesus was humble and yet, all-powerful. Humility is not weakness; it's strength under control. Humility recognizes we have authority only because we're *under* authority. When we stay safely under God's authority in all parts of our lives, we can walk in confidence, knowing His all-powerful authority protects and guides all parts of our lives.

Humility doesn't mean beating yourself up. Humility is the opposite of devaluing yourself. Seeing yourself through God's eyes is actually the highest view of human life you can have. Seeing yourself the way God does gives you the opportunity to live with so much freedom. See, pride isn't a sin because it causes you to think too big; it's a sin because it actually tricks you into a prison of thinking far too small.

When you do fall because of pride, know you don't have to be defined by that defeat. Have the humility to admit fault, seek forgiveness, learn from your mistake, and start walking in God's wisdom. Pride is the enemy of wisdom, but humility is the fast track to wisdom.

PRAYER FOR TODAY

———————

Father, please forgive me of my sinful pride. Help me walk in the humility of knowing that You're in control. Help me walk in confidence because I know that confidence is actually a gift from You, but pride is a sinful counterfeit for confidence. Please help my heart stay humble and teachable. Don't let me get pressured to be like the crowd or like anybody else in the chase for popularity. Thank You that Your presence in my life guides me along the path of wisdom. Please keep me on that path, and don't let pride ever sabotage Your plans and purposes for me. Help me have a heart like Jesus.

In Jesus's name, amen.

Humility is not weakness; it's strength under control.

DAY 8 *May 27, 2023*

Sexual Purity

———

"Sex is a gift to be shared with a spouse, not with a stranger. It's a gift to enjoy passionate intimacy with your spouse in a lifelong marriage, but sex with anyone else causes harm. Enjoy the pleasures of sexual intimacy in marriage, but don't be intoxicated or tempted into sex with anyone who is not your spouse."

Proverbs 5:17–20

You live in a world of sexual temptation, and the decisions you make about sex will have a huge impact on your future. The path of wisdom will keep you from the scars of sexual sin, but the path of foolishness will cause you to ignore God's word and make compromises. In His grace, God forgives us when we do fall, but sexual sin still creates some wounds and baggage that can have a lifelong impact.

Several years ago, it was time to have a serious talk about sex with my oldest son. Ashley and I have always been candid with the boys, trying to take the shock and scandal out of sex conversations. In age-appropriate ways, we try to keep an open dialogue around changing bodies and hormones, mixed messages about sex in culture, and God's plan for sex in Scripture. We want to be the first place our kids turn to when they have questions about sex instead of starting with Google or friends.

All these little conversations along the way finally culminated in the granddaddy of all sex talks. Unsure if I was ready or if he was ready, I'd put it off long enough. After I had done my best to awkwardly explain the mechanics of intercourse, the beauty of God's design for sex within marriage, and the warnings of misusing the gift of sex outside of marriage, I worked up some forced enthusiasm and said, "Hey, buddy! What did you think about that? A lot of good info, huh?"

As I turned to see his response, he had his head buried by his knees with his hands over his head. He had the posture of someone who was puking on an airplane. I waited a moment to make sure he hadn't actually puked. Then I waited another moment to make sure I wasn't going to puke. Neither of us puked.

We both regained our composure, laughed off the awkwardness, and launched into meaningful conversations about God's perfect plan for the gift of sex and how that plan has been hijacked, misused, and redefined by a culture searching for meaning and pleasure apart from God. We talked about the joy of sex when expressed within a healthy marriage and the negative aftermath of sex when used casually. We talked about how sex should always be rooted in respect.

Sex is a powerful gift when enjoyed within marriage, but it creates powerful pain when misused outside of marriage. Sexual sin may feel good in the moment, but temporary pleasure is never worth the permanent regrets it causes.

When we choose to misuse sex outside of marriage, we disrespect ourselves, our partner, and the God who created sex and created us in His own image. Everyone gets hurt as a result. When respect for God's laws, respect for our own bodies, and respect for others is at the forefront of our thinking, we'll no longer ask, "How far can I go without getting into trouble?"

Instead, we'll ask, "How can I show more respect to myself, to my future spouse, to my Creator, and to people He has made in His own image?" If we'll take that approach, we'll be able to enjoy the standard for sexuality the apostle Paul gave to all Christians when he said, "Among you, there must not be even a hint of sexual immorality" (Ephesians 5:3).

PRAYER FOR TODAY

———

Lord, in a world where I'm surrounded by sexual temptation, confusion, and mixed messages surrounding sex and sexuality, help me choose to trust Your Word even more than I trust my own feelings. I know that everything You ask me to do is for my good, for the good of others, and for Your Glory. Help me honor You with my body and with my thoughts related to sex. I pray for my future spouse that they would also make wise choices and stay on Your path of wisdom in a world of sexual brokenness. Thank You for creating the gift of sex. From this moment forward, help me commit my thoughts and my actions to living in line with Your standards for sexual purity.

In Jesus's name, amen.

Sexual sin may feel good in the moment, but temporary pleasure is never worth the permanent regrets it causes.

DAY 9

Always Be Generous

"Generosity leads to prosperity. Those who bless others will themselves be blessed."

Proverbs 11:25

God wants you to live a generous life. Generosity isn't just about money. Chances are that in this season of your life, you don't have much (or any) money, but you can still be generous with what you do have. If we'll look at what we do have, we'll find there are always opportunities to be generous. I started donating blood at our local blood bank when I was a teenager because, at the time, it was literally the only thing I had to give.

You can be generous with your time. You can be generous with your service. In the years to come, when you do have more money, you can be generous with that as well.

It seems strange on the surface, but in God's economy, giving is its own form of receiving. The backward value systems of the world tell you to get all you can. God tells you to give all you can. We might think that generosity will lead to an empty bank account, but godly generosity is a pathway to prosperity. This prosperity doesn't only refer to finances (although financial blessings can be part of it). God's prosperity is a richness of joy and peace that could never be measured in only dollars and cents.

Jesus was the perfect model of God's generous heart. Jesus sacrificed His position of glory and comfort in heaven to enter our world of brokenness and pain. He sacrificed the wealth of heaven for a life of poverty. He sacrificed His time on earth to serve the needs of others instead of claiming His right to be served. He gave His life on the cross to pay the price of sin that was our debt to pay and not His.

In living a supernaturally generous life, He received much more than He lost. He gave His life, but He was resurrected to eternal life. He suffered temporary pain, but it paved the way for us to experience eternal glory with Him. God has a way of taking our generous gifts offered in faith and multiplying them like seeds in a fertile field yielding 30, 60, or even 100 times what we originally gave in the harvest.

Generosity also invites joy into your life. Think about the most joyful people you know. I'll bet they're generous people. Now, think about the most generous people you know. I'll bet they're also joyful. Think of joy and generosity as the two wings on the same bird. Once you choose one, you realize the other is attached, and your life begins to soar.

If you'll remember that everything we have (including our lives) belongs to Jesus, and we are only temporarily managers of it, then we'll be free to faithfully give when God nudges us to give. When we honor God and serve others through the generosity of our time, talents, and treasures, blessings always follow. Commit today to live a life of generosity. It's one of the wisest decisions you'll ever make.

PRAYER FOR TODAY

Jesus, thank You for giving everything for me. Help me live my life with the same generous Spirit You have. Lead me and guide me toward the faithful generosity of my time and my resources. Help me be a blessing to others. Please show me where I can best use my time and talents to serve others. Let me never love money or possessions more than I love You and people. Help my priorities be in line with Yours. Please help me experience the joy and freedom that generosity always makes possible. Thank You for Your goodness and grace.

In Jesus's name, amen.

Think of joy and generosity as the two wings on the same bird. Once you choose one, you realize the other is attached, and your life begins to soar.

DAY 10

Choose Your Friends Carefully

"If you want to be wise, then spend time with wise people. If you want to get into trouble, then hang out with troublemakers."

Proverbs 13:20

The book of Proverbs teaches us that a true friend can be even more loyal than a brother or sister. We all crave friendships with that kind of loyalty. Helen Keller was blind and deaf, and I imagine that forging meaningful friendships required her (and her friends) to work through significant communication barriers and other obstacles. She faced life-long hardships and adversity, but she recognized that the gift of good friends makes life more beautiful. She once said, "So long as the memory of certain beloved friends lives in my heart, I shall say that life is good."

One of the most important decisions you can make in this season of your life is choosing what kind of friends you want to have. Your parents have probably given you plenty of advice already about choosing your friends wisely, and maybe you rolled your eyes or even ignored their advice. But their advice about choosing friends wisely is more important than you can possibly imagine. Few things have more power to shape your future (for good or for bad) than your friends.

One of the greatest distinctions between a wise life and a foolish life is in how we choose our friends. When we value personality over integrity, we're being foolish. When we keep chasing after selfish friends trying somehow to win their praise and loyalty, then we waste our energy. Proverbs teaches us that a true friend will stick to us closer than a brother. This is the kind of friend we need to be and the kind of friend we need to seek.

Your life will start to look like the lives of your closest friends. If you choose to spend time in the company of wise friends and mentors, you'll find their wisdom contagious. If you hang out with people who don't share your values, you'll find that their compromised set of values will start rubbing off on you. Jesus was a friend to all, but He was also very intentional about choosing His inner circle. We must be very intentional as well.

Choosing our friends wisely is not an excuse to become snobby or to act like we're better than anyone else. In fact, the right friends will help us to become more humble and more willing to serve others from all walks of life. Healthy relationships fuel us, and when we prioritize time alone with Jesus and time together with close friends who share our faith and values, we'll become the best version of ourselves. "Just like iron sharpens iron, true friends help sharpen each other" (Proverbs 27:17).

Our friends have a great influence on our lives. Especially in moments of temptation and the crossroads decisions of life. The wrong voices might enable unhealthy habits, while a true friend will provide loving accountability. The wrong voices might cause you to compromise your character, while a wise friend will help you achieve even higher levels of character and integrity.

To have wise friends, we must first commit to being a wise friend. Start where you are by living with integrity at school, at home, online, and in all parts of your life. Wise words and wise actions attract others who want to live with wisdom. When we speak and act with selfishness, foolishness, and a disregard for God's Word, then we'll draw peers who share those same mindsets. Be intentional. You will stay on the path of wisdom much easier if you have the right friends on the journey with you.

PRAYER FOR TODAY

―――――――

Lord, thank You for being my truest friend. Thank You that You never leave me or forsake me, even when others have. Help me be a true friend to You and help me connect with others who will be true friends as well. Give me the wisdom to discern who should be part of my inner circle. Help me choose friends who will increase my wisdom and not friends who might sabotage my wisdom. Protect me from negative influences and help me never be a negative influence to others.

In Jesus's name, amen.

To have wise friends, we must first commit to being a wise friend.

DAY 11

The Power of Your Words

"Kind words diffuse anger, but harsh words instigate fights."

Proverbs 15:1

Your words have more power than you probably realize. Every word you speak to your parents, your siblings, your teachers, and your friends—even the words you post on social media all carry weight. The words you choose and the tone of those words have the power to build people up or tear people down. The tone of your words will shape the tone of your life. Choose a positive one.

In Jesus's famous Sermon the Mount, He gives special praise to the "peacemakers." In every situation, you have the unique opportunity to either make peace or instigate tension. Let your default mode be one of peace. Be slow to anger and slow to take offense. Don't stir up drama. Choose to believe the best in people and their motives. Look for common ground wherever you can. Your school, your home, and everywhere you go should be better places because of the words you speak.

To find common ground and diffuse tense situations, your ears are as important as your mouth. The more you listen, the more credibility you'll have when you speak. Pride will tempt you to shout until people hear your point, but the humble path to wisdom will give you the discipline to lean in and listen. I know you have a lot you can teach, but remember that you (like all of us) still have a lot to learn. Seek to win friends more than you seek to win arguments.

The Bible tells us that the power of life and death is in the tongue. Our words have immense power to tear down or to build up. God created the entire universe using only the power of His words, and then He created us in His image, giving us power in our words too. Be a peacemaker. Use this power for good and not for evil.

While our default mode should always be set to peace, like the example of Jesus correcting the fight-picking Pharisees, there will be moments in life when we *must* speak up and correct others. In these delicate moments, we must be simultaneously humble and bold. The boldness is rooted in a desire to speak the truth even when it requires courage to say it. The humility comes from a sincere desire for even our corrective words to ultimately build others up.

If we'll allow the Holy Spirit to fill our hearts and guide our steps, He will give us wisdom with our words in these moments when we might not know what to say. If you live surrendered to God, He will empower you with the wisdom you need in every conversation. Wisdom is not the same as eloquence, so don't feel the need to make your words poetic. Simply speak the truth and do it with love, and you'll be on the right track.

PRAYER FOR TODAY

—————

Father, thank You for entrusting me with such power and influence with my words. Help me use my words to build up and not to tear down. Please forgive me for all the careless words I have spoken in my life. I know I've done damage both intentionally and unintentionally. Please help me not cause pain in the future and bring healing to the damage I've already caused. Give me courage when I need to speak with boldness. Give me humility when I need to receive correction or simply listen and learn instead of spouting off my own opinions. Thank You for the love and patience You have for me. Help me have this same love and patience for others.

In Jesus's name, amen.

The tone of your words will shape the tone of your life.

DAY 12

There's No Real Success
Without God

---

*"People are always making their own plans, but the Lord is
the one who gives the right answers. People think all their
own ways are right, but the Lord is the only accurate judge
of our hearts and motives. Commit all your plans and all
your work to the Lord, and He will be the one who ensures
your success."*

Proverbs 16:1–3

When I was in school, I always thought the "Most Likely to Succeed" superlative was a bizarre award to give to someone. The truth is, every person has a 100% chance of success if they choose to follow God. That success might look different from the world's superficial definitions of the word, but God's definition of success is the only one that really counts. If you'll follow God's plan, then you'll succeed. It's that simple.

Some people treat *God's Plan* like a mystical and unknowable force. They go through life making plans and giving little thought to God until they come to a crossroads and don't know which way to proceed. They ask for God's guidance more as a superstitious exercise than a sincere act of devotion and faith.

Other times, people proceed with their own plans, not even pausing to consider whether or not God might be directing them. They move forward with cavalier confidence and then pray as an afterthought, asking God to bless what they've already decided to do.

We've all been guilty of these kinds of broken mindsets related to God's will. Some of our mistakes come from an innocent misconception about what God's plans are all about. The good news is, God's will for your life is not as complicated as you might imagine it. Ultimately, He wants you to love Him, love other people, and develop your character to reflect the heart of Jesus.

You might be asking, "But what about the big life decisions? Which job should I take? Which college should I attend? Which person should I marry? Doesn't God care about these parts of my life?"

The thing is, His version of success might look different than your own. The "success" He has planned for your life is more about your character than the specific outcomes and goals you've set for yourself. Even a season of struggle and disappointment can produce great "victories" in God's eyes if those struggles bring you closer to God and make your heart more like the heart of Jesus.

God cares about the details of your life even more than you do. He loves you even more than you love yourself. When you come to these decisions, He wants to guide you, but He also wants you to realize those bigger aspects of His will. If you'll make it your daily mission to grow in your love for God and people, and stay rooted in Christ, then the Lord will be able to direct you toward everything He has for you.

When you are walking with Jesus, you're always headed in the right direction. Even if you happen to take your eyes off him and get sidetracked, in His grace, God can get you back on the right path. Yes, you still need to make plans and make decisions, but you should always remember that God works in you, and He is the one who will ultimately bring success. "The warhorse is prepared for the battle, but the Lord is the one who brings the victory" (Proverbs 21:31).

PRAYER FOR TODAY

———

Lord, thank You that You care about every detail of my life. Thank You for loving me so much. Please guide me in all life's decisions. Give me peace about which way I should go. Remind me that Your will for my life is primarily about my relationship with You. Help me put You first in everything, and shape my heart like Yours. I commit myself into Your hands. Take my dreams, my plans, my goals, and my very life as an offering to You. I know any success achieved apart from You isn't real success. I want Your will and not my own.

In Jesus's name, amen.

When you are walking with Jesus, you're always headed in the right direction.

DAY 13

Peace Is Better than Wealth

"Eating leftovers in peace is far better than a houseful of feasting with conflict."

Proverbs 17:1

When you imagine your dream home, what do you picture? For most of us, we're conditioned by TV shows and social media images to dream of a home with fancy finishes, spacious yards, and immaculate cleanliness. While those physical attributes of a house can bring certain comforts, the Bible calls us to a much richer vision of home life. We're reminded that a shack filled with peace and love is infinitely better than a mansion filled with strife and drama.

We all desire peace in our homes, but peace can be an elusive quest if we don't go about finding it in the right way. We tend to think of peace as simply referring to the absence of conflict. This is an incorrect and incomplete definition of the Hebrew notion of "shalom" (peace) as described throughout Proverbs and all of the Old Testament Scriptures. Shalom isn't referring to the absence of something nearly as much as the presence of something.

We will experience God's peace when we make Him the authority over every part of our lives. His authority brings protection and wholeness. Apart from His authority, we trade in the wholeness He gives in exchange for the chaos that reigns whenever we don't follow God's laws. Any part of your life lived apart from God's principles will eventually create chaos. Give every part of your life to Jesus, and He will bring His peace.

Take an inventory of your life, your home, and your relationships. Identify the areas where there seems to be more chaos than peace. Which places seem to have more brokenness than wholeness? In those areas, you must declare God's authority and invite Jesus (The Prince of Peace) to reign supreme. When Jesus leads your words, thoughts, actions, hobbies, goals, motives, and relationships, you will have peace in your mind and in your life.

It's important to recognize that the presence of peace isn't a guarantee against conflicts or even tragedies. We still live in a broken world, and the storms of life will rage against us at times. But if your life is firmly fastened to a foundation of faith in Christ, you will endure life's storms. Even through tears and scars, God's peace can continue to reign supreme, and you can sleep in peace at night, knowing God is bigger than anything you will face tomorrow.

PRAYER FOR TODAY

———

Jesus, I invite You to reign as the Prince of Peace and the King of Kings in all parts of my life. I know I can't truly experience real peace without Your presence and Your grace. Please forgive me for the ways I've allowed my own sin and selfishness to sabotage peace for myself and for others. Help me trust You through the storms of life. Help my faith in You inspire faith in others. Help me be an instrument of Your peace in my relationships and in my home.

In Jesus's name, amen.

We will experience God's peace when we make Him the authority over every part of our lives.

DAY 14

The Poison of Porn

"Guard your eyes. Don't be led astray by lust."

Proverbs 6:25

One of the most difficult challenges of adolescence and young adulthood is to keep your thoughts pure in a world of visual, sexual temptation. As a teenager, I fell into sin in this area and developed a toxic habit of looking at pornography. Allowing my eyes and my thoughts to feed on lust was one of the most self-destructive mistakes I've ever made.

Our world will try to tell you that whatever happens in your thoughts doesn't really matter. They'll tell you it's nobody's business but your own. They'll tell you it's just harmless entertainment, and your fantasies don't hurt anybody. The truth? Lust destroys. Porn poisons the mind and heart and sabotages relationships. Porn also fuels the demand for human trafficking, sexual slavery, and sexual abuse. It's not "harmless" entertainment. It damages both the viewers and the actors in countless ways.

Even if you don't watch porn or sexually explicit "entertainment," lusting after other people is sinful and damaging. Lust warps your mind to look at people as nothing more than objects who exist for your pleasure. It creates a prison keeping you away from healthy relationships with God or with other people.

Jesus gives us these same warnings. He taught that to lust after somebody or to replay sinful fantasies in your mind is already a sexual sin even if you never actually touch that person. The Bible has so much to say about our thought life. Your thoughts shape your attitudes and your actions. You might feel powerless over your thoughts, but you have more power than you realize.

You're the one who decides what images you watch on TV or on your phone. You decide what thoughts you allow to replay in your mind. You decide whether to keep your sin secret or to seek accountability. Choose to honor God, honor yourself, and honor others (including your future spouse) by committing to pursuing sexual purity in your thoughts and in your actions.

Lust is certainly a temptation, but you never need to feel ashamed for feeling tempted. God created you to be a sexual being, and that strong sex drive is actually a wonderful gift from Him—as long as it's enjoyed within marriage. Don't settle for counterfeit forms of pleasure.

If you've already fallen into a sinful cycle of lust and/or porn, you don't have to stay stuck there. Ask God for forgiveness and then take immediate action to get accountability through tools like monitoring software on your devices and internet activity. You also need to confess the struggle to a trusted mentor who can help provide accountability. God never calls us to get through a struggle on our own. He is there to help us, and He also wants us to gain strength from friends, family, and mentors who can help us. You're not alone.

PRAYER FOR TODAY

Lord, thank You for creating me with a healthy sex drive that makes me look forward to the gift of sex in marriage someday. In the meantime, please help me guard my eyes, my thoughts, and my actions. Help me protect sexual purity in myself and in others. Forgive me for the ways I've failed in this area, and please help me renew my mind with Your Word and recommit to a thought life where lusting is not welcomed.

In Jesus's name, amen.

Choose to honor God, honor yourself, and honor others (including your future spouse) by committing to pursuing sexual purity in your thoughts and in your actions.

DAY 15

Your Temper Is a Tempter

"Don't befriend hotheads. Don't spend your time with people who are always angry and offended. Angry attitudes can become contagious, and you might start adopting their bad habits."

Proverbs 22:24–25

We all experience anger sometimes, and what we choose to do with that anger can either help us or hurt us. Once when I was a teenager, I got so angry that I punched a wall. The only thing my angry outburst achieved was making my hand sore for days. It was an unproductive expression of anger that caused pain and embarrassment instead of healing.

You must learn to master your anger, or else your anger will master you. Anger itself is not a sin, but it can certainly lead to sin. Sometimes, anger is the appropriate response, but it's never the appropriate *mindset*. Jesus experienced anger, but He never sinned. When He saw the money-changers exploiting and extorting people in the name of God, He kept his mindset right and responded appropriately with righteous rage. Jesus got angry when He saw injustice, hypocritical behavior, and abuse. When you see people exploiting and taking advantage of others, that is when God calls you to master your anger and respond appropriately. When your focus changes from protecting others or healing a situation to exploding or wallowing in your anger, that is when you and your anger stand on dangerous ground.

Unfortunately, some people choose to live with an angry mindset, seeing themselves as a perpetual victim. They scoff at all those who disagree with them. They shut their ears to wisdom. They want to punish others but never allow anyone to correct or discipline them. The book of Proverbs bluntly calls this mindset foolish. Unchecked anger will make a fool of you, and foolishness is a contagious condition. Some people pretend to be passionate, but really their passion is just a mask for unchecked anger.

As Christians, God calls us to be kind to all people, but He also calls us to have wisdom and discretion in choosing our close friends. Bad company corrupts good character. If you always make excuses for a hot-tempered friend, eventually, their temper will create unnecessary problems in your own life. Your desire to bail them out might come from compassionate motives, but your actions do more harm than good. Let them face the natural consequences of their actions, or they'll never learn.

Much anger stems from unmet expectations and broken views of ourselves. When we replace those mindsets with a spirit of gratitude and closeness to God, His ways start to become our ways, and anger will slowly be replaced by peace. If you have an ongoing problem with anger, then develop the daily discipline to express gratitude to God for all the good in your life. Get alone with Him to meditate on His Word and let Him remind you that He loves you just as you are.

PRAYER FOR TODAY

Lord, please help me have a heart like Yours. Let only the things that anger You anger me, and help me have the wisdom to respond appropriately. Please forgive me for the sinful and angry mindsets I've carried. Help me replace those mindsets with Your truth and Your wisdom. Please let Your peace fill my heart so that my first instinct to unmet expectations is no longer anger but peace rooted in Your presence and promises. Please give me the wisdom to know which relationships are causing contagious anger in my life and show me how to create safe boundaries to protect everyone involved. Help me be a peacemaker in a world full of rage.

In Jesus's name, amen.

You must learn to master your anger, or else your anger will master you.

DAY 16

Pay Attention to the Right Voices

"Pay attention and listen closely to the sayings of the wise; turn your heart to what I teach. It's a gift when you keep wisdom in your heart and have wise words ready on your lips. I'm teaching you this wisdom so that your trust will be in the Lord."

Proverbs 22:17–19

This Scripture begins with two simple words you've probably heard often from your parents and your teachers, "Pay attention." When Proverbs tells us to pay attention to the sayings of the wise, it's a call to refocus on what really matters. Whatever captures your attention will eventually influence your direction. When I tell my own sons to pay attention, I want to help them snap out of the stupor of mindlessly escaping into video games or to stop feeding on the mental junk food our culture makes available 24/7. I need this reminder in my own life too. We never outgrow the need for reminders to pay attention to what really matters.

We have a real enemy in the world. Satan isn't a guy wearing red tights with a pitchfork. He's a deceiver who subtly tries to discourage us and distract us from God's plans and promises. When left to drift on autopilot, we all become susceptible to numbness, discouragement, deception, and distraction from the world's messages. We need to wake up!

Stop paying attention only to the messages of this world. Stop giving in to your own doubts, worries, and uncertainties. Stop shaping your worldview solely by what you see on social media and television.

We must also pay attention to the right advisers. Solomon's son Rehoboam split the kingdom through his foolish pride by not listening to the sage advice of older advisers. He only trusted his peers, who told him what he wanted to hear. The results were disastrous. We must seek the voices of the wise and allow them to speak into our lives. "A nation will crumble with a lack of guidance, but with many wise counselors, there is success" (Proverbs 11:14).

Above all voices, we need to pay attention to God's promises and commands. God is the only perfect advisor whose advice will always be correct. Get alone with Him. Turn off the noise of the world. Refocus your thoughts on His promises. You're doing this right now simply by carving out time to take part in a Bible-based devotional. Let this good decision you've already made today give way to others.

God is always at work. Pay attention to what He does all around you. He promises that we'll find Him when we seek Him with all our hearts. He wants you to find him. He's waiting, putting evidence of His presence all around you, showing you opportunities to serve others for His glory, and inviting you to join Him in world-changing work. The opportunities are there if you let prayer lead you and pay attention to His promptings.

PRAYER FOR TODAY

Father, thank You for Your love. Thank You that You don't make Your wisdom a mystery to us, but You show us in Your Word what You desire and how we should live. Help me pay attention today. Help me clearly see what You're doing all around me. Help me walk the path of wisdom and not be distracted by the world's false messages. Help me see and choose the narrow road of wisdom and life instead of the broad road of destruction. Thank You for guiding me.

In Jesus's name, amen.

Whatever captures your attention will eventually influence your direction.

DAY 17

Protect the Powerless

———

"Never take advantage of the poor. Never exploit the needy in court. The Lord is the defender who will take up their case, protecting their rights and opposing all those who would abuse or disregard the poor."

Proverbs 22:22–23

One of my big regrets from my youth is a time I saw a friend of mine being bullied in the locker room at school, and I didn't do anything to step in and stop it. My fear of being bullied in return kept me paralyzed from having the courage to do the right thing. God calls us to protect the powerless. Anytime we see injustice or see someone being mistreated, we should be willing to step in and protect those who can't protect themselves.

Our world seems to reward the strong and mistreat the weak, but God's value system is different from the world's value system. When the prophet Samuel was searching for the next King of Israel, he overlooked the scrawny shepherd boy named David in favor of other men who looked the part. The Lord reminded Samuel that while the world may look at the outer appearance, God is not impressed with superficialities. God looks at the heart.

One of Jesus's most sobering parables was the story of how God would ultimately divide the righteous from the unrighteous based on how they had treated the poor and marginalized. Jesus tells us that whatever we do for the poor (whether it's helping them or exploiting them), we're ultimately doing it to Him. He's bluntly telling us that we can't say we love Him while having complete disregard for our brothers and sisters in need.

To have a heart like Jesus, we must be willing to care for people the world might overlook. There's no such thing as an insignificant person to God, so there should be no such thing as an insignificant person to us. All are precious in His sight and made in His own image. In Jesus' earthly ministry, He showed us the heart of God for the poor, the powerless, the disenfranchised, the imprisoned, the forgotten, and the marginalized.

In different ways and in different seasons of our own lives, we've all fallen into one or more of these categories. We've all been spiritually or financially poor. We've all been overlooked. We've all experienced injustice. In those moments of our own powerlessness, what we prayed others would do to help us is exactly what we should be doing to help others.

Use whatever influence you have to help those without influence. Use your voice to speak for those who can't speak for themselves. Recognize that your resources (even your very life) don't belong to you. They all belong to God, and He has temporarily entrusted them to your stewardship. Manage those resources well to provide for your own family but also to remember the needs of the poor. One of the purest acts of faith is doing good for those who can do nothing to repay us.

"Speak up for the voiceless. Ensure justice for the oppressed. Stand up for the helpless and make sure they receive justice" (Proverbs 31:8–9).

PRAYER FOR TODAY

———

Jesus, please help me see Your face in the faces of the people I'm tempted to overlook. Help me see the dignity and sacred value in every human being, especially those the world has de-valued. Don't let me get caught up in the world's superficial popularity contests. Please give me a heart to help those in need. Give me discernment to know how I can best help and let me never be part of the problem instead of part of the solution. Thank You for loving me even in my own spiritual poverty and giving Your life on the cross for me though I could do nothing to repay You. Your love inspires me to love. Your compassion inspires compassion within me. Through Your Holy Spirit, please equip me to be a voice to the voiceless and to be Your hands and feet to a world in need. Let my simple acts of service point more people to Your heart. Guide my life toward opportunities where I can make a difference for those who need it most.

In Jesus's name, amen.

There's no such thing as an insignificant person to God, so there should be no such thing as an insignificant person to us.

DAY 18

Financial Freedom

———

"Don't make expensive commitments or get yourself deep into debt. If you start missing payments, you could end up losing everything you have."

Proverbs 22:26-27

I got a credit card when I turned eighteen. It proved to be my most foolish choice. I started charging things without thinking about how I would pay for those purchases with interest attached to it. I had to dig myself out of a hole of debt over the next few years, but it was all avoidable if I had just applied God's financial principles right from the beginning. So many teenagers ignore God's principles for their finances, and as a result, they dig themselves deep into the kind of debt that can take years to overcome.

Most modern advertising is designed to sell us stuff we don't need and can't afford. Since marketers are good at their jobs, many of us have taken the bait and bought stuff we don't really need. Once you are paying all your own bills, you will likely quickly learn the painful lesson that no possession is worth a lack of peace. Debt can become a form of slavery, and God wants you to live with freedom.

When God warns us against unnecessary debt, it's not to limit us. Like all God's guidelines, it exists for our protection, for our freedom, and to help us live the full and abundant life Jesus brings us without inhibitions. When we take on debt, we limit our family's future freedom. When we choose to live with fiscal discipline, we're making an investment into our family's future freedom.

When we choose discipline today, we're free to live with generosity and abundance in the future instead of selfishness and scarcity in the future. Every wise financial decision we make creates future opportunities, but every foolish financial decision removes future opportunities. Make financial choices today that your future self will thank you for making.

Some people have misinterpreted the Bible to say that money is evil. Actually, the Bible says the love of money is the root of all kinds of evil, but the Bible also tells us that God has given us the ability to create wealth and the responsibility to manage resources with wisdom. Poverty and wealth are not sins. Wealth is not a sin. Worshipping money, misusing money, or trading your freedoms in exchange for unnecessary debts are sinful.

When we allow God's Word to be our chief financial advisor (as well as our chief advisor in all areas of life), we walk the path of wisdom. God wants you to have peace in your finances. The Bible tells us God wants you to be able to leave an inheritance to your grandchildren. If you want a financial legacy of peace, prosperity, and kingdom-minded generosity, then submit to the Bible's money principles instead of the broken pattern of greed and discontentment we see in the world.

PRAYER FOR TODAY

———

Lord, help me trust You with my finances. I recognize that all money belongs to You, and whatever I have is only temporarily entrusted to me. Help me manage those resources wisely. Thank You for giving me the strength and ability to earn an income. I know I don't have much money of my own right now, but help me be faithful with the little I do have so You can someday entrust me with more. Help me someday create a multi-generational legacy of financial freedom for my family and help me remember that my self-worth has nothing to do with my net worth.

In Jesus's name, amen.

Every wise financial decision we make creates future opportunities, but every foolish financial decision removes future opportunities.

DAY 19

Develop Your Skills

"Being skilled and disciplined in your work opens doors of opportunity. Those who excel in their field will work along-side leaders and those with great influence."

Proverbs 22:29

Your primary responsibility in this season of your life is to develop your skills. Students who squander these years set themselves up for future difficulties and disappointments. Students who make the most of these development years give themselves a huge head start toward future opportunities. The size of your opportunities tomorrow depends on the size of your efforts today.

The Bible has so much to teach us about work. It teaches us not to seek our identity in work because a job title or the grades we make can't define us. It also teaches us that work is important. When done with excellence, it can be an act of worship. God wants us to give every task, every assignment, and every opportunity our very best effort. Strive to maximize your potential by developing the skills God gave you.

The passage from Proverbs challenges us to work hard at what we do and work hard at getting better. Don't settle for less than your best. You might milk the timeclock and still get paid by just going through the motions, but you'll never get ahead that way. You might be able to make good grades without ever really giving much effort, but you should always give your best. You know when you've given your best effort regardless of what grade you might receive.

It's good to do your best and set goals for yourself, but watch out for the kind of ambition that can lead to pride. Ambition can become dangerous when fueled by selfish and prideful motivations, but ambition can be a very good thing when we have pure motives. God wants His children in positions of leadership and influence. He wants our good deeds to shine before others so that we may use that influence to serve the needs of our communities and point people toward the goodness of God.

Start seeing your home, your school, and your job (if you have one) as sacred places. They are every bit as sacred as a church service on Sundays. You are a temple of the Holy Spirit. Jesus lives within you from the moment you reach out to Him in faith and receive His grace. Jesus goes with you into that job. Jesus goes with you into your home. You're representing Christ in everything you do. Once you realize this truth, everything you put your hands to becomes sacred work, and you'll want to continue to excel at it for God's glory.

PRAYER FOR TODAY

Lord, thank You for giving me unique skills and abilities. Please give me the discipline to develop those skills. Help me to keep improving in all parts of my life. Don't let prideful motivations creep in and attempt to wreck what You're doing through me. In all things, help me work with a pure heart seeking to please You more than I seek to please any human boss or teacher. Please give me more influence in my work, my school, and in my community, and help me leverage that influence for others' good and for Your glory.

In Jesus's name, amen.

The size of your opportunities tomorrow depends on the size of your efforts today.

DAY 20

Beware the Party Crowd

"Listen to wisdom, my children, and get your hearts in the right place. Don't go partying with people who are addicted to alcohol and overindulgence. Gluttons and drunks become poor, and laziness is their legacy."

Proverbs 23:19–21

Chances are good that there are kids in your school already experimenting with alcohol. Regardless of whether or not you believe drinking is acceptable behavior for adults, the Bible teaches us to obey the law of the land, which means nobody under age twenty-one should drink at all. The Bible also warns that being drunk is dangerous, foolish, and reckless. So many teenagers have made poor life-altering (or even life-ending) decisions under the influence of alcohol.

A few verses after the passage above, we see this strong warning about the dangers of drunkenness: "Who has headaches? Who has regrets? Who has animosity? Who has stress? Who has heartache? Who has anger? Who has bruises and bloodshot eyes? It's those who love to frequent bars. It's those who are always looking for a drink. Yes, the drink might feel good for a moment, but in the end, it leaves you hurting. Your vision will be blurry; your mind will be foggy. You'll feel seasick like a sailor in a storm. You'll have an arrogant and dangerous mindset that says, 'Go ahead and hit me! I can't feel a thing. I'm bulletproof. Where can I find another drink?'" (Proverbs 23:29–35)

In this season of your life, alcohol is unwise, unsafe, and illegal. When your peers go down that road and try to make it seem like the cool thing to do, remember that God has called you to live with health, honor, and wisdom. God has called you to live a world-changing life, and it's not worth sabotaging God's plans by hopping in with the party crowd.

If you've already gone down the drinking road and perhaps you feel stuck in a bad habit, then reach out for help. Admitting you need accountability and help isn't a sign of weakness; it's a sign of strength and wisdom. Don't stay stuck in a cycle of sin and shame. Jesus came to give you freedom, but don't use your freedom to justify unhealthy behaviors or habits. God wants to set you free from anything that holds you back from the freedom Jesus gave His life to give to you.

Be aware of friends and loved ones who might be falling into dangerous habits with alcohol. Be careful not to make them stumble deeper into negative habits. Be willing to ask difficult questions and point out troubling patterns. Those conversations are not easy, but Proverbs tells us that one of the hallmarks of a true friend is someone who loves enough to speak a difficult truth.

PRAYER FOR TODAY

———

Lord, thank You for the freedoms You've given us. Please never let me misuse those freedoms and become imprisoned by unhealthy habits. Let no addiction take hold of my family or me. Don't let me get caught up in negative peer pressure and surround me with friends who share my faith and values. Please give me the wisdom to stay accountable, realizing that anyone can fall into addiction without true accountability. If I ever do find myself in a place where a habit has become an addiction, please help me see it clearly and have the strength to reach out for help. Help me also be a source of strength to my friends and family and never one who causes them to stumble into sin.

In Jesus's name, amen.

God has called you to live a world-changing life, and it's not worth sabotaging God's plans by hopping in with the party crowd.

DAY 21

Honor Those Who Have Sacrificed for You

―――

"Keep learning from your father; he gave you life. Don't push away your mother when she is old. Pursue truth, wisdom, and insight as great treasures worthy of great sacrifice. The parent of a righteous child has a joyful heart. A parent's greatest treasure is having a child grow in wisdom and integrity. May your parents experience this kind of rich blessing as a result of your choices."

Proverbs 23:22–25

One of the most practical ways to practice wisdom in this season of your life is to show honor and respect to your parents. Apart from our Heavenly Father, no parent is perfect; but we should respect all parents. Despite every parent's inherent imperfections, when we give them our lifelong honor and respect, we put wisdom into action and secure a multi-generational blessing.

As this passage from Proverbs points out, part of honoring our parents is living a life of honor and integrity. When you choose to embody the positive lessons they taught you, they experience a rich blessing and the fulfillment of the dreams and prayers they've had for you since before you were born. Honor your parents and honor God by choosing to live a life of integrity and wisdom.

Another aspect of honoring your parents is forgiving them. Your parents aren't perfect. They made mistakes. Perhaps some of those mistakes caused you a lot of pain. Forgiveness doesn't excuse sin, but it trusts those past wounds into God's hands and allows healing in your own heart and in your relationships with those who hurt you. If you have the power to rebuild a broken bridge to your parents, then be the one to start extending grace. In doing so, you walk the path of wisdom. Even if a parent has been absent all your life, instead of letting bitterness or insecurity take root in your heart, choose to lean into the loving presence of your heavenly Father, who has never left your side.

Your parents (and other mentors in your life) have done much more for you than you've seen with your own eyes. The prayers they prayed for you and the sacrifices they made for you have blessed you in ways you could never calculate or adequately repay. You stand on the shoulders of giants. Give them honor. Show them gratitude. Live a life of integrity, and you'll make their hearts happy. You'll also honor your Father in heaven.

PRAYER FOR TODAY

———

Father, please help me honor You and honor my parents through my gratitude, respect, and integrity. Help me live a life that becomes an answer to the prayers they prayed for me. Help me forgive them for the ways they failed by showing them grace and compassion and remembering that You, Father, are the only perfect parent. Thank You for my parents and for the mentors You placed in my life over the years. I know there have been countless sacrifices made on my behalf and countless prayers prayed for me. Give me a spirit of gratitude when I reflect on those sacrifices and help me live in a way that brings honor to my family and glory to You.

In Jesus's name, amen.

Honor your parents and honor God by choosing to live a life of integrity and wisdom.

DAY 22

Always Tell the Truth

"An honest answer is as sweet as a kiss."

Proverbs 24:26

Choosing to be an honest person is one of the most important choices you will ever make. An honestly earned B (+ or -) is better than cheating to get an A. Choosing honesty (even when it costs you something) honors God, displays integrity, and shows wisdom. The world will tempt you to put on an act in what you say, in what you do, and in what you post on social media, but rise above those temptations and choose to be real and honest. God has no greater joy than to see His children walking in truth.

One of the main themes in Proverbs is the importance of honesty in all parts of life. The Scriptures cover everything from honesty in business to honesty in courtrooms to honesty in relationships. The poetry of this verse from Proverbs uses the word "kiss" to remind us that honesty means more than just having the right facts. Honesty is an expression of love. The honest answer is always the right answer.

Since the truth requires love, we must be careful not to speak cruelty cloaked in truth. Honesty does not give you a license to critique everyone. Be an encourager. The world has plenty of critics already. Let your words be true but let them also be loving, encouraging, and compassionate.

Being loving and kind doesn't mean you'll never have to share a difficult truth. Proverbs also tells us that a true friend will sometimes have to speak hard truths—hard to say and hard to hear. In those delicate moments, be honest and direct, and make sure you solely base your motives on helping your friend. You must also be humble enough to hear honest words of correction when you need them. Honesty requires humility both in how we speak and in how we listen.

Honesty is also not a license to gossip or to have unfiltered conversations about others. True, maybe you heard something about someone's life, but that does not give you license to share it. Don't be a gossiper, and don't befriend gossipers. Anyone who will gossip to you will also gossip about you.

We might try to hide the motives of our gossip behind an artificial desire to help someone, but gossiping is always dangerous. The book of Proverbs has many blunt warnings for those who would justify gossip. Other scriptures simply point out the consequences of it, like the Proverb that states, "A fire dies out without wood to fuel it, and fighting dies out without gossip to fuel it" (Proverbs 26:20).

PRAYER FOR TODAY

———

Lord, thank You for your unwavering honesty. You are the Way, the Truth, and the Life. You, Jesus, are the very embodiment of Truth. Please help me live my life walking in the path of truth and honesty. Forgive me for the times I've lied and shown cruelty with my words or gossip. I know words and motives have power, and there have been times my words and my motives have been impure. Thank You for Your grace. Help me commit my words and my motives to Your perfect standard of truth even when the truth costs me something. Let me never fear the sacrifices that I must sometimes make in the pursuit of truth and integrity.

In Jesus's name, amen.

The honest answer is always the right answer.

DAY 23

Criticism Won't Kill You

"To the one who listens and learns from it, constructive criticism is as valuable as solid gold."

Proverbs 25:12

Nobody likes to hear criticism, but at times, correction is a refining fire that can help strengthen us and burn away our imperfections. One of the primary distinctions between the wise and the foolish is in how they handle criticism. Foolish and immature people will get angry at any form of correction, but a wise person will use the critique (regardless of the critic's motives) to become even wiser.

When a teacher, parent, or coach corrects you, don't take it as an insult; take it as helpful instruction meant to make you better. When someone with mean-spirited motives criticizes you (or even insults you) online, behind your back, or even to your face, don't let those mean words define you. Most of those critical words aimed at you are caused by brokenness in the critic and not at all because of any brokenness in you.

If you desire to have influence in any part of life, you must know this: Criticism is the price of influence. The more influence you attain, the more criticism you will have to endure. Many people have hidden from their life's calling simply because they did not have the courage to endure the criticism that will always come when we step out in faith into all God has for us.

Even though you'll probably have to endure criticism from others, don't retaliate by throwing harsh words at those who speak harsh words to you. Show respect even to those who don't deserve it, not as a reflection of their character, but as a reflection of yours. Be an encourager. The world has plenty of critics already.

Avoiding criticism is a futile effort because even if you hide from it, criticism will find you. In a world full of scoffers, critics, haters, and know-it-alls, everyone seems to have an opinion (usually a negative one) about almost everything. We can be dragged down by this pervasive negativity, but we must also train our ears to find the important truths hidden within the criticism.

There are essentially two types of critics. The first type has no motive except to hurt you. Their words are like daggers, and they want to discredit you and discourage you. Remember that these negative people are usually wounded in some way, and the negativity they direct toward you really just masks their own internal wounds. Pray for these people, but don't let their words make you second-guess your calling or your abilities.

The second type of critic is the person who cares about you and wants you to get better. These people invest in you and only want good things for your future. They usually have pure motives, even when their words might seem harsh. Guard your heart when you hear their correction, and don't get discouraged. At the same time, have the humble spirit to learn from their perspective. Learn to see your own blind spots. Learn to be teachable. The moment you stop listening to correction is the moment you stop growing.

PRAYER FOR TODAY

———————

Father, first and foremost, help me always remain teachable when it comes to the correction You bring into my life through the Holy Spirit and the truth of Your Word. Let me humbly receive the loving correction You bring to all Your beloved children. Also, help me remain open to constructive criticism from other people. Never let me grow discouraged because of the negativity of haters, but also let me never close my ears to the constructive correction I need to hear. Help me be thankful and not defensive when someone has the courage to offer me constructive criticism. Help me be an encourager instead of a critic. Help me remain teachable and continue growing through every season of life.

In Jesus's name, amen.

Be an encourager. The world has plenty of critics already.

DAY 24

Be Sensitive to Those Who Are Hurting

———

"Trying to force a grieving person to cheer up is as insensitive as taking away someone's coat in a snowstorm or pouring vinegar into a wound."

Proverbs 25:20

Sometimes it's hard to know what to do or what to say when a friend or loved one goes through a really hard time. There's a time to cheer up a discouraged friend, but when a loved one is in a time of intense sadness, you need you to honor their pain. Honoring someone's pain means acknowledging their season of deep difficulty and choosing to help them through it by being present. It means letting them set the emotional tone. When they feel like laughing, laugh with them. When they feel like crying, be a safe place for them to share their tears.

A good friend of mine lost his wife to cancer, and in an instant, his dreams crumbled, his bride was gone, and he suddenly became a single father of two young children. He and his wife were both only twenty-nine-years-old when it happened—tragedy can strike at any age. The first year after her death was so painful, he didn't know if he could make it through another day. Many people did their best to encourage him, but few could relate to his tragedy.

When I later asked what had helped bring him the most hope during his darkest days, he said, "When someone is hurting, don't try to cheer them up by telling them it's going to be okay. Just be with them in their pain until *they're* ready to say it's going to be okay."

He described the ministry of presence. In our most painful moments, we gain strength by the presence of our loved ones. Don't avoid your loved ones who are hurting. Don't let not knowing what to say intimidate you. There is power in presence. In our pain, we rarely remember the words people say to us, but we never forget who showed up to be there with us.

Just texting a friend to let them know you are thinking of them or praying for them can go such a long way. A willingness to sit with a friend and let them share their story is sometimes all it takes to bring hope to somebody who feels hopeless. Sometimes showing love is as simple as reaching out or showing up.

If you're in a season of pain, know that God is with you. The Scriptures promise that He is especially close to the brokenhearted. He comes on a rescue mission for us when our hearts feel broken, and our souls feel crushed by the weight of tragedy. He also promises to wipe every tear from our eyes and one day set all things right and make all things new. Because of Jesus, all our pain is temporary, and all our joy will be eternal.

If you're in a season of pain, please also extend grace to your friends. Pain can warp our thinking and make us quick to take offense at our friends' absence or their inability to take our pain away. People are flawed and imperfect. Choose to believe the best of your loved ones in your moments of pain, even if they don't show up for you in the ways you want them to. You never know all they might have to carry in their own life. Jesus is the only perfect friend. Everyone else (including you) will disappoint their friends at times.

Don't run from someone else's pain, and don't run from people when you are in pain. Healing happens in community. We need God, and we need each other. When we carry each other's burdens, the load gets much lighter.

PRAYER FOR TODAY

Jesus, thank You that You came to earth and experienced sadness and pain and that You can relate to us in grief. Thank You for being present with me in my own pain. Help me to be present and encouraging to my friends and relatives when they grieve. Give me the courage to be present with them in their pain and to be an extension of Your hands and feet in their life in those important moments. Help me to be a good friend and help me have good friends in my time of need. Thank You for being a friend who is always there for me.

In Jesus's name, amen.

In our pain, we rarely remember the words people say to us, but we never forget who showed up to be there with us.

DAY 25
Learn from Your Mistakes

"Just like a dog will return to its own vomit, a fool will return to his foolish choices."

Proverbs 26:11

This verse is intentionally graphic in its description of a disgusting action. If you've ever owned a dog, then you've probably seen your pet puke and then lick it up again as if it has somehow become a delicious snack. It's super gross. As humans, the thought of this sickens us, but this Scripture reminds us that through our repeated sins, bad habits, and foolish mindsets, we perpetually return to something even more repulsive than vomit. This vivid imagery is a wake-up call.

You might imagine that this verse primarily pokes fun at other people's foolishness and not our own. That wouldn't be consistent with Scripture since even Jesus warned us to be aware of the plank of wood in our own eye before we worried about picking out the speck of sawdust in someone else's eye. This verse doesn't poke fun at the foolishness of others nearly as much as it causes some sobering self-assessment in our own lives. What proverbial vomit do you keep returning to? What unhealthy habits do you need to change?

Sometimes our unhealthy habits and foolish quirks are more obvious than others. If you deal with an addiction of some kind, the imagery of this verse might hit uncomfortably close to home. Perhaps you know your issue well, but you can't seem to pull away from it. You may even feel a sense of self-loathing and helplessness tied to the action, and yet, you can't seem to break free. In cases like these, you need to reach out and get help. The only foolish way to deal with an addiction is to think you can beat it on your own. Get the help you need to break free.

Other times, our repetitive and self-destructive habits are harder to spot. They may be tied to a mindset. Perhaps your thoughts get on a mental loop of negativity, and the "vomit" in your situation is a thought process keeping you stuck in a cycle of negativity. In those cases, you must take your thoughts captive and renew your mind with the truths of Scripture. Meditate on God's Word instead of fueling your mind with the world's toxic mindsets. Have a long period of silence and stillness in your day where God can do His work without competing with all the noise of the world.

Remember that every sin begins in the mind, and every positive action begins in the mind too. You must be the gatekeeper of your mind, choosing which thoughts and images are allowed to enter and which ones must leave. God will help you in this mental exercise if you'll let Him. Like all parts of life, you don't have to do it alone. The Holy Spirit is there to guide you, strengthen you, and empower you.

PRAYER FOR TODAY

Lord, please forgive me for all the ways I've struggled with repetitive sins and foolish habits. Please help me break free. Please bring conviction to help me clearly see the blind spots that hide the toxic parts of my life and my mindset. You gave Your life to set me free, so don't let me throw away my freedom by staying stuck in sinful habits. Guide me toward healthier thoughts and habits. Help me stay committed to positive habits such as daily time alone with You through prayer and reading from Your Word. Thank You for caring about every detail of my life.

In Jesus's name, amen.

What proverbial vomit do you keep returning to? What unhealthy habits do you need to change?

DAY 26

Don't Pick Fights

———

"Inserting yourself into someone else's argument is as foolish and reckless as yanking a wolf's ears."

Proverbs 26:17

My great-aunt, Pearl, lived to be 103-years-old. When she turned 100, we threw a big birthday party for her, and the local news showed up to do a story on her. The reporter asked Aunt Pearl the secret to a long life. She thought for a second and then laughed out loud and said, "I suppose one of the secrets is to mind your own business!"

Aunt Pearl had some wisdom there. Certainly, as followers of Jesus, He calls us to sometimes get involved in other peoples' situations. Especially when we see someone bullying someone else or someone suffering pain or injustice, we should spring into action to provide whatever help we can. Injustice and suffering are always our business when we have the opportunity to help.

However, this Proverb doesn't warn us against helping people who need help. It's warning us against the pride of thinking that we have the right to pick fights, give unsolicited advice, or correct others as if we're the authority on every topic. We live in a time when social media has made it easier than ever to think everything is our business and every topic is an opportunity for us to start arguments, correct everyone whose opinions differ from our own, or make every single issue "our business."

Wisdom helps us listen and serve others much more quickly than we correct or confront others. The only appropriate time to insert yourself uninvited into someone's situation is when you are ministering and not meddling. Knowing the difference between the two can be complicated sometimes. Jesus gives us a vivid example of what uninvited ministering looks like in his famous parable of the good Samaritan. In the story, bandits beat, rob, and leave a man for dead. Several religious leaders passed by the bloody victim on the road, but they chose not to get involved. A foreigner from Samaria, with plenty of excuses not to stop, decided to selflessly serve this victim by sacrificing his own time and financial resources.

Jesus hailed the Good Samaritan as the quintessential example of what it means to be a good neighbor and to show love for others. When given the opportunity to selflessly serve, we should always do it. When we see someone in desperate need, and we have the power to help, we must put our faith in action and help.

The difference between the Good Samaritan scenario and inserting yourself into someone else's affairs in a negative way largely comes down to your own motives. When selfish pride motivates you, you'll find yourself feeling entitled to correct others. When love motivates you, you'll find yourself feeling compelled to serve others. Love brings healing and unity, but pride brings destruction and division.

Don't let argumentative people bait you into senseless fights and arguments. Be kind even to unkind people. Your kindness doesn't reflect their character. Your kindness reflects God's character. He is loving and patient with all of us, even at our worst moments. As ambassadors of Christ on earth, make it your mission to be like Him in all situations.

Jesus was the perfect example of knowing when to intervene and when to stay out of an argument. He helped all those in His path who needed His help. He lovingly taught everyone who came to Him with a desire to learn, but He also never fell into the trap of wasting His time and energy debating with people who only wanted to argue. When people tried to entrap Him in no-win situations, Jesus would always show love and speak truth, but He also showed the wisdom and restraint to walk away.

When you see someone who needs your help, let love lead you to help. When you see someone tempting you into an argument, let wisdom lead you to walk away. When you're not sure whether a complicated situation requires your intervention or your absence, ask the Holy Spirit to guide you. When you allow God's principles and His Spirit to guide your heart, you'll have discernment in those moments.

Do your best to live at peace with all people, but recognize that some people will refuse to live at peace with you. In those cases, pray for them and love them from a distance. Don't sink to the level of those who want to sling mud. Always take the high road.

PRAYER FOR TODAY

———

Lord, in a world with so much outrage, please help me to be an ambassador of peace. Help me have the courage to help those who truly need my help. Help me have the wisdom and restraint to walk away from arguments that don't concern me. Guide my steps, my words, and my actions. Thank You, Jesus, for the perfect example You gave to us through Your own life. Let Your Holy Spirit guide me to make those same wise decisions and use my life to point others toward You in the process.

In Jesus's name, amen.

When you see someone who needs your help, let love lead you to help. When you see someone tempting you into an argument, let wisdom lead you to walk away.

DAY 27

Let Others Do Your Bragging for You

———

"Don't brag about the future since you don't know what will happen tomorrow. Let other people do your bragging for you. If you sing your own praises, you'll be singing a solo."

Proverbs 27:1–2

The world's definition of success seems tied up in endless self-promotion. Many of the lyrics of popular songs and social media posts of popular celebrities seem to be filled with self-praise and bragging. Jesus modeled a much different kind of greatness than the superficial bragging celebrated by the world.

We are called to serve people and not to impress people. We are called to make Jesus's name famous instead of only striving to make our own names famous. We are called to be not only the most confident people on earth but also the most humble. We have confidence because we know our identity in Christ, but we have humility because we know only Christ is perfect, and we still have a lot of growing to do.

God bases His definition of success on our faithfulness and not our fame. When we buy into the world's version of success, we'll look for every imaginable opportunity to brag, name-drop, and shine the spotlight on our personal brands because we think that's what it takes to get ahead. When we find rest and peace in God as the keeper of our life and purpose, we'll have the confidence to reject the superficial rituals of the world.

Most bragging, at its core, is a cry for validation from a broken and insecure heart. Ironically, we act most puffed up when we feel most empty inside. When we see others bragging, our initial response might be to roll our eyes and pass judgment on their immaturity. While we shouldn't approve of anyone's bragging, we should also have compassion. Most bragging stems from brokenness much more than it stems from pride.

Perhaps your parents didn't love or validate you as a child. Maybe you feel like no one in your life truly sees you and celebrates you, so you have to shine the spotlight on yourself. Please know that God sees you, and He loves you. Keep reminding yourself of your identity in Him, and His love will guard your heart. He has great things in store for you, so don't sabotage His plans by pursuing validation from others more than you're pursuing your destiny in Christ.

Chasing the world's definition of success, we might end up as braggarts and approval junkies, hoping the applause of the world will somehow make up for the emptiness we feel when we've been ignored or criticized by others. What you and I need to remember is that no amount of praise for the world can ever fill that void. Only God can fill that void. Ultimately, only God can fulfill every desire for approval in your heart, and He already loves you unconditionally. He is the source of our wholeness.

Once you've decided to root your identity in Christ, you'll find yourself far less impacted by the world's praise or the world's criticisms. You won't have the same need to receive credit or praise. You'll be content to do your work faithfully, knowing God sees it all and His opinions of you count more than the combined weight of all the world's opinions.

God loves you. Let that sink in. He sees you. He knows every detail of your life. He's seen you at your very best and your very worst, and He loves you more than you can possibly imagine. Once that fully sinks in, it will set you free.

If you do anything worth bragging about, others will eventually do your bragging for you. It will be a much more compelling endorsement of your work coming from others' lips and not your own. When you brag on the work of others instead of yourself, you'll find your choice of encouraging and cheering others on will bring joy to them and to you as well. Don't spend your whole life chasing the fickle praise of this world when you already have the unending love of God.

PRAYER FOR TODAY

———

Lord, thank You for loving me. Help me root my identity in Your love and not in the opinions of others. Forgive me for the times I've let my sinful pride motivate me to brag and hog the spotlight. Help me walk in humility, to point the spotlight back on You, and to encourage others. Help me to rest, comfortable in Your love, knowing Your opinion of my work is the only one that counts for eternity. Help me pursue wisdom more than fame and service more than spotlights.

In Jesus's name, amen.

Once you've decided to root your identity in Christ, you'll find yourself far less impacted by the world's praise or the world's criticisms.

DAY 28

Confession Brings Healing

———

"People who try to cover up their sins and scandals will not prosper, but if they confess and turn from them, they'll find mercy."

Proverbs 28:13

When I was a teenager, a friend introduced me to pornography. I didn't have a smartphone or even home internet at the time, but that exposure hooked me into an ongoing habit of looking at porn whenever I had the opportunity. I knew it was wrong, but my pride lied to me and told me I'd be better off if nobody knew about my struggle. My cowardice kept me from confessing to my parents or to any friends or mentors who could provide accountability and help. My pride kept me imprisoned for far too long and caused me much harm, all because I resisted confessing and tried to deal with it all on my own.

God's plan for healing always involves relationships (both our relationship with Him and with others). When selfish pride motivates us, we'll be tempted to protect our image at all costs, and we'll push away healthy relationships that would bring accountability. When our image becomes threatened because of our sin and imperfections, it tempts us to shift blame and spin the story instead of humbly admitting fault. Confessing and apologizing for our mistakes requires courage and wisdom. Making excuses or blaming others for our mistakes is a sign of cowardice and foolishness.

The Bible gives us many examples of those who have chosen wisely and others who have chosen foolishly when confronted with their own sin. A foolish example is when a married couple in the book of Acts named Ananias and Sapphira get caught in a lie. Instead of confessing, they continued to perpetuate the lie. Their stubborn dishonesty and pride cost them their very lives. Their story is a sobering reminder that a refusal to speak the truth and accept personal responsibility carries consequences.

A positive example in the Bible is when a courageous young woman named Rahab decided to turn from her sinful life of prostitution to align herself with God's principles. She left a life of dishonor, and God greatly honored her as a result. She risked her life to help God's people attain a strategic military victory. Eventually, she married and became the matri-arch in a line of Israel's greatest kings. She's even listed in the earthly lineage of Jesus Himself.

The world's response isn't always the best indication of God's response. The world's response will often mirror God's merciful principle, but some-times they don't match. We've seen times when a leader or celebrity is constantly caught up in scandals for which he or she never takes respon-sibility, yet they continue to rise in power or popularity. There are other times when someone will humbly admit fault with sincere repentance and still become the victim of cancel culture or other forms of targeted harassment.

The Bible tells us that these types of injustices will happen in life. It also tells us not to get discouraged when the wicked prosper or when we see injustice of any kind. God has an eternal mindset and will one day set the temporary injustices of our world right, once and for all. Following God's plan (even when it comes at personal cost) will ultimately bring an eternal return of blessings.

We will experience some of those blessings in this life, but we will experience them in their perfect fullness in heaven. Live with that eternal perspective. God will always make good on His promises to reward those who confess and renounce their sin and to hold those accountable who conceal and deny their sin. Choose to trust Him. Know that the Lord will honor our faithfulness even when the world dishonors it.

PRAYER FOR TODAY

———

Lord, give me the humility to recognize fault. Give me the courage to admit fault. Don't let sinful pride cloud my judgment and sabotage Your plans for me. Help me extend grace to myself and also to those who have wronged me. Help me have the faith to forgive even those who have never asked for forgiveness. Holding a grudge only hurts the one who holds it, so help me live freely. Forgive me for all the ways I've committed and concealed sins. Help me choose a new path. Thank You for Your forgiveness and grace.

In Jesus's name, amen.

Confessing and apologizing for our mistakes requires courage and wisdom. Making excuses or blaming others for our mistakes is a sign of cowardice and foolishness.

DAY 29

Think Before You Speak

---

*"There is nothing more foolish than to speak before
thinking about your words."*

Proverbs 29:20

My mom was a hospice nurse, meaning she cared for people at the end of their lives. Once someone gets close to death, their greatest joys and their greatest regrets come into clear focus. For many people at the end of life, their greatest regrets had to do with words they spoke in anger that hurt their loved ones. They recognized the power and lasting scars caused by those words and wished they could go back in time and never say those hurtful things.

In the New Testament, Jesus teaches that we will all be held accountable for every word we've ever spoken. He warns that our words will have the power to condemn us or to acquit us. As part of the greater gospel story, we know that only Christ Himself and our faith in Him has the power to save us, but that doesn't take away the personal responsibility we have for our words. Jesus clearly wants us to see that our words matter deeply, and every word we ever speak, text, or post matters.

The power of our words is a repeated theme throughout all Scripture. From the beginning of time in Genesis, the Bible teaches us that God used His words to speak the universe into existence. He then created us (men and women) in His own image, giving us power in our words as well. We must use the power of words for good and not for evil. We must use our words to build each other up and not tear each other down.

The solution isn't to live as mute monks, afraid to speak for fear of sinning. We must have the courage to engage in meaningful dialogues, but we must also understand the power of words and the damages that an undisciplined mouth can do. Not every thought you have needs to be verbalized. Not every opinion you have needs to be posted on social media. There is wisdom in speaking a timely word, but there's also wisdom in knowing when to not speak at all.

Part of being a wise peacemaker means walking away from an argument instead of insisting on being heard. Wisdom often requires restraining your emotion instead of using your heightened emotions to give fuel to thoughtless words. As Proverbs also tells us, "Fools give full vent to their anger, but wise people quietly restrain their anger" (Proverbs 29:11).

This doesn't mean we should never confront others. There are certainly times when a situation needs confrontation. Jesus wasn't afraid to confront others, and we shouldn't be either. But in those moments, remember that motives matter. If you want to confront someone just to put them in their place or to make your own voice heard, then you stand on dangerous ground. If you have pure motives to protect everyone involved and preserve relationships by establishing healthy boundaries, then strong words are probably appropriate.

In all situations, think before you speak. Ask yourself, "Is what I'm about to say true, kind, and necessary?" Speak the truth in love. Speak with wisdom. Speak humbly. Remember that your words have power, and your speech is a direct reflection of your heart.

PRAYER FOR TODAY

Lord, thank You for giving us so much power in our words. You've trusted us with a great responsibility. Please help me have the wisdom to use the power of words in a positive way. Forgive me for all the times I've spoken with impure words or impure motives. Let every word I speak, text, or post honor You and be used to build others up. Help me always practice the discipline of thinking before I speak.

In Jesus's name, amen.

There is wisdom in speaking a timely word, but there's also wisdom in knowing when to not speak at all.

DAY 30

The Foundation of Your Life

"All God's promises are true. All people who trust in Him are secure."

Proverbs 30:5

When my older boys were little, they kept trying to build a fort out of old boxes, boards, and sticks in the woods near our house. At first, they built it on the muddy ground with nothing but gravity. The fort kept collapsing every time a storm came through, so I told the boys to rebuild their fort on a solid foundation. If the foundation was solid, with everything tied together securely, their fort could survive the storms.

At the end of Jesus's famous Sermon on the Mount, He summed up His teachings by giving the illustration of wise and foolish builders. The wise builder put His house on a solid foundation. The foolish builder put his house on an unsteady foundation. Both houses looked good from the outside, but when the storms of life raged, only the house built on a solid foundation was left standing.

The moral of Jesus's story is that our lives are built on a foundation. We must choose whether we build our lives on a foundation of God's promises or if we will trust in the shifting sands of our own feelings or cultural whims. Faith in God anchors us through life's storms and ties everything together securely. Storms in life are inevitable, but destruction is optional. Trusting in God is what makes all the difference.

There have been followers of Christ throughout the ages who have withstood relentless storms by holding onto an even more relentless faith. In her book, *The Hiding Place*, Corrie Ten Boom recounts her life inside a concentration camp during the Holocaust where Nazis sent her for hiding Jewish families. She talked about the abhorrent conditions in the camp. Despite the abuse she endured, she refused to complain and decided to trust God's promises.

She even trusted the Scripture that commands us to give thanks in all situations. Some of the other women asked her how she could thank God for the putrid smells, fleas, and disease in their filthy barracks. She replied that the filthy conditions kept the guards outside so that the women inside had the freedom to openly praise God, pray, share conversations, laugh, and experience some measure of dignity and privacy.

When we choose to trust in God's promises, we will start to see God's blessings when others can see only curses. We will see opportunities for ministry where others see only limitations. We will see opportunities for gratitude and joy where others see only excuses to complain and feel discouraged.

Trust in God's promises because they all hold true. You'll find strength in God's promises when you hide His Word in your heart. Take time to meditate on God's Word. Memorize His Word. Build your life on a foundation of His Word, and your life will weather any storm.

PRAYER FOR TODAY

Lord, thank You for keeping Your word. Thank You that all Your promises hold true. Thank You that You are the foundation where I can build my life and my hope for eternity. Thank You, Jesus, for the sacrifice You made for me. Help me trust You with every detail of my life. Please forgive me for the many times I've taken my eyes off You and become discouraged. Remind me of Your faithfulness so I might cling to faith through all life's storms. I know You're always holding me.

In Jesus's name, amen.

Storms in life are inevitable, but destruction is optional. Trusting in God is what makes all the difference.

DAY 31

Real Beauty Comes from Within

"Charm is superficial, and beauty is temporary, but a woman who trusts the Lord will be celebrated. Honor her for all she has done. Let everyone esteem her noble lifestyle."

Proverbs 31:30–31

You're growing up at a time of mass confusion about issues related to gender. Depending on where you go to school and what messages you hear, you've probably been told many things about what it means to be a man or a woman, which aren't at all based on reality. God made us either male or female, and our gender is a God-given, unchangeable gift, part of His unique destiny for our lives.

God created both genders with dignity, honor, and eternal worth, but unfortunately, one of the most obvious places where the world's broken value system can be seen is in the unfair treatment of women and girls. Through all kinds of sexist practices through the centuries, women have been objectified and valued through a skewed, superficial lens. The book of Proverbs saves its final words to make it clear that God honors women—and everyone else should as well.

In the secular world, one of the most common misconceptions about Christianity is that it teaches a worldview that holds women down. The truth is, no one, throughout all of human history, has done more to elevate women than Jesus did during His life and ministry. In radically counter-cultural ways, Jesus empowered women through His words, friendship, example, grace, healing, and teachings—He intentionally highlighted female heroes in many of His parables.

As Christians, we should lead the movement of honoring women. We need to honor women for their character and not simply for superficial qualities like physical appearance. Real and lasting beauty isn't measured by outward appearance; it's measured by internal character, faith, and integrity.

For ladies, Proverbs 31 calls for you to receive honor, but it's also a roadmap for the type of life and work God sees as most worthy of honor. It's a life of integrity and hard work. It's a life of selfless service. It's a roadmap showing girls what kind of woman they should aspire to become.

It shows boys what kind of woman to pursue in marriage someday and how to honor her when you do. If you'll apply these wise principles from Proverbs, you'll build a solid foundation for your future marriage, your future family, and every other aspect of your future.

PRAYER FOR TODAY

Lord, help me live out the message of Proverbs 31. Help me celebrate honorable women and men and to strive for that kind of honor in my own life. Please never let me base my identity on superficial things. Please help me pursue wisdom in my relationships and lead me to a future spouse who lives out these wise principles. Let every part of my life and my future honor You as I strive to be a man or woman of honor, integrity, and wisdom. Thank You, Jesus, for the wisdom and the grace you give to us. Guide me by Your Holy Spirit to walk with You all the days of my life.

In Jesus's name, amen.

Real and lasting beauty isn't measured by outward appearance; it's measured by internal character, faith, and integrity.

NEXT STEPS

Congratulations on reaching the end of this book! In a world that tempts people to quit everything early, you've shown perseverance by completing this book, and that says a lot about your maturity and your character. You're clearly wise beyond your years, and I'm praying for you and cheering you on as you continue pursuing wisdom and God's plans for your life.

I pray this book is only the beginning of your journey in applying God's wisdom to every part of your life. As you continue to study God's Word, I challenge you to read one chapter from Proverbs each day as part of your daily Bible reading. In just a few minutes of reading per day, you'll complete the 31 chapters of Proverbs once per month. This daily discipline can have a profound impact on your faith, and each time you re-read the wisdom of the Bible, the Holy Spirit will bring His Word to life in fresh ways for you. I started this practice as a teenager, and it's changed my life. If you do it, it will be life-changing for you as well!

In addition to Proverbs, please explore the rest of the Bible too. The book of Psalms and the Gospels (stories about Jesus—the books of Matthew, Mark, Luke, and John) are a good place to start and a good place to keep returning. We all have our favorite places in the Bible, but make sure you explore the totality of God's Word from Genesis to Revelation. Every word of the Bible is God-breathed, timeless, powerful, and practical to help you in every part of life. Keep treasuring God's Word, and your life will become a blessing to Him and to others as you grow more like Jesus every day.

Remember the decisions you make in this season of your life shape the person you'll become and the opportunities you'll have in your future. Keep choosing the path of wisdom, and don't settle for anything less than God's plan for you. When you've blown it (like we all do sometimes), remember that Jesus is ready to offer forgiveness and help you restart on the right path. God has such extraordinary plans for you, and when you walk with Jesus, you're always headed in the right direction.

ACKNOWLEDGMENTS

This book was birthed from a collective effort with many friends, mentors, and ministry partners. I want to personally thank some of the people who have made this book possible.

First of all, I want to thank my extraordinary wife, Ashley. She's the heart of our home, and next to God's grace, she's by far the greatest gift the Lord has ever entrusted to me. Next to Jesus, she's also the one most responsible for leading me along the path of wisdom by her example, her love, her prayers, and her encouragement. While this is one of the few books that has my name on it and not hers, her wise influence can be felt on every page. I love you, Sweetie.

I'd also like to thank our dear friends and ministry partners, Brent and Stephanie Evans. Their vision and leadership made this book possible, and their encouragement and guidance have helped shape every page. This book would not exist without them. It's a privilege for Ashley and me to serve with them and with the entire extraordinary team at XO.

Through the years, the path of wisdom has been shown to me through the authentic example of countless friends and mentors. Some of these people influenced me through close relationships, and some impacted me from a distance as I watched them live their lives in a way that honored God. I want to thank all those who have left me better than they found me through their authentic faith and wisdom. This list of mentors and influencers is far too great to share by name (because I'd end up forgetting people and then feeling guilty about it), but I do want to specifically thank my parents, Brad and Karen Willis, who have shown me the path of wisdom and love through their authentic examples from the time I was born.

I also want to thank YOU for taking the time to read this book and intentionally building your own faith and wisdom. You are clearly wise beyond your years by investing the time this early in your life to grow in wisdom. In your own life, remember that every word you speak and every choice you make has the potential to shape your future and to impact those around you. When you choose the path of wisdom, you're not only blessing your own life; you're also being used by God to lead others in the right direction.

Finally, and most importantly, I want to thank our Lord and Savior, Jesus Christ. He is the true source of all wisdom, truth and life. Thank you, Lord, for your unending grace. Thank you for inviting us to join you on a journey that leads to eternal life. Please guard our hearts and guide our steps along the path of wisdom as we follow you.

ABOUT THE AUTHOR

Dave Willis is a pastor, writer, and marriage ministry leader. His books, blogs, videos, podcasts, social media channels, and live events have reached millions of people worldwide. Dave and his wife, Ashley, are also part of the team at XO Marriage—the nation's largest marriage-focused ministry. Dave and Ashley have four wonderful sons and one spoiled puppy.

For additional resources, please visit daveandashleywillis.com or xomarriage.com.